THE IMPORTANCE OF

F. Scott Fitzgerald

These and other titles are included in The Importance Of biography series:

THE IMPORTANCE OF

F. Scott Fitzgerald

by Gail B. Stewart

Lucent Books, P.O. Box 289011, San Diego, CA 92198-9011

Library of Congress Cataloging-in-Publication Data

Stewart, Gail, 1949–
      The importance of F. Scott Fitzgerald / by Gail B. Stewart.
          p.   cm. — (The importance of)
      Includes bibliographical references and index.
      Summary: Discusses the life, work, and significance of the
  noted American writer who authored such works as "The
  Great Gatsby" and "This Side of Paradise."
      ISBN 1-56006-541-9 (lib. bdg.)
      1. Fitzgerald, F. Scott (Francis Scott), 1896–1940—Juvenile
  literature.   2. Authors, American—20th century—Biography—
  Juvenile literature.   [1. Fitzgerald, F. Scott (Francis Scott), 1896–
  1940. 2. Authors, American.]   I. Title.   II. Series.
  PS3511.I9Z8715   1999
  813'.52—dc21   98–50387
  [b]   CIP
                                                            AC

Copyright 1999 by Lucent Books, Inc., P.O. Box 289011,
San Diego, California, 92198-9011

Printed in the U.S.A.

Contents

Foreword

THE IMPORTANCE OF biography series deals with individuals who have made a unique contribution to history. The editors of the series have deliberately chosen to cast a wide net and include people from all fields of endeavor. Individuals from politics, music, art, literature, philosophy, science, sports, and religion are all represented. In addition, the editors did not restrict the series to individuals whose accomplishments have helped change the course of history. Of necessity, this criterion would have eliminated many whose contribution was great, though limited. Charles Darwin, for example, was responsible for radically altering the scientific view of the natural history of the world. His achievements continue to impact the study of science today. Others, such as Chief Joseph of the Nez Percé, played a pivotal role in the history of their own people. While Joseph's influence does not extend much beyond the Nez Percé, his nonviolent resistance to white expansion and his continuing role in protecting his tribe and his homeland remain an inspiration to all.

These biographies are more than factual chronicles. Each volume attempts to emphasize an individual's contributions both in his or her own time and for posterity. For example, the voyages of Christopher Columbus opened the way to European colonization of the New World. Unquestionably, his encounter with the New World brought monumental changes to both Europe and the Americas in his day. Today, however, the broader impact of Columbus's voyages is being critically scrutinized. *Christopher Columbus*, as well as every biography in The Importance Of series, includes and evaluates the most recent scholarship available on each subject.

Each author includes a wide variety of primary and secondary source quotations to document and substantiate his or her work. All quotes are footnoted to show readers exactly how and where biographers derive their information, as well as provide stepping-stones to further research. These quotations enliven the text by giving readers eyewitness views of the life and times of each individual covered in The Importance Of series.

Finally, each volume is enhanced by photographs, bibliographies, chronologies, and comprehensive indexes. For both the casual reader and the student engaged in research, The Importance Of biographies will be a fascinating adventure into the lives of people who have helped shape humanity's past and present, and who will continue to shape its future.

IMPORTANT DATES IN THE LIFE OF F. SCOTT FITZGERALD

1896

Born on September 24 in St. Paul, Minnesota.

1898

Family moves to Syracuse and Buffalo, New York, when his father gets a job with Procter and Gamble.

1908

Edward Fitzgerald loses his job; the family moves back to St. Paul.

1911

Because of poor grades, Fitzgerald is sent to Newman Academy in New Jersey.

1913

Fitzgerald enters Princeton University.

1914

His script for *Fie! Fie! Fi-Fi!* is accepted by the Triangle Club at Princeton; he meets and falls in love with Ginevra King.

1915

Poor grades make him ineligible for the Triangle Club show; in November he leaves Princeton, knowing he will soon be suspended.

1917

Having returned to repeat his junior year, Fitzgerald once again leaves—this time to join the army; *The Romantic Egotist* is rejected.

1918

While stationed at Camp Sheridan in Montgomery, Alabama, he meets and falls in love with Zelda Sayre.

1919

He is discharged from the army and gets an advertising job in New York; Zelda breaks their engagement; he moves to St. Paul to finish his novel *This Side of Paradise;* it is accepted by Scribner's in September.

1920

This Side of Paradise is published in March; in April he and Zelda are married in New York.

1921

The Fitzgeralds visit Europe for the first time; their daughter, Frances "Scottie" Fitzgerald, is born in October.

1922

His second novel, *The Beautiful and Damned,* is published; they move to Great Neck, Long Island.

1923

He writes a play, *The Vegetable,* which flops in Atlantic City.

1924

They decide to economize by moving to the French Riviera; Zelda has a brief affair with a French aviator.

1925

The Great Gatsby is published in April while the Fitzgeralds are in Europe.

1927

Fitzgerald gets a job writing a screenplay in Hollywood, where he meets Lois Moran; in March he and Zelda move to Ellerslie, near Wilmington, Delaware.

1928

Zelda becomes obsessed with ballet dancing; they spend the summer in Paris and return to the United States in the fall.

1930

Zelda suffers first breakdown in April while they are in Paris.

1931

Zelda recovers slowly; by September her doctors allow her to return to the United States.

1932

Zelda suffers second breakdown; Scott moves into La Paix, a house near her hospital.

1933

Fitzgerald's drinking worsens; he finishes *Tender Is the Night.*

1934

Zelda breaks down for the third time; Fitzgerald, in despair over her illness and lack of money, suffers from poor health as well as alcoholism.

1935

He goes to Asheville, North Carolina, to try to recuperate.

1936

Fitzgerald writes "The Crack-Up," describing his collapse.

1937

He gets a job in Hollywood as a scriptwriter.

1938

He finishes script for *Three Comrades,* but it is unsatisfactory.

1939

He begins *The Last Tycoon.*

1940

In November Fitzgerald suffers a small heart attack; he dies on December 21, after another heart attack, and is buried in the Rockville, Maryland, Union Cemetery.

Praise, Scorn, and Pity

By the time of his death at age forty-four, F. Scott Fitzgerald had published four novels and 160 stories. His name had become synonymous with the 1920s Jazz Age. Critics hailed his first book, *This Side of Paradise,* published when he was only twenty-four, as brilliant. The *New York Times Book Review* of May 9, 1920, praised Fitzgerald's "delightful literary style," observing that "the glorious spirit of abounding youth glows throughout this fascinating tale."[1]

A "Cracked Plate"

In the last years of his life, Fitzgerald's name was no longer praised. One had to look very hard—and often with little success—to find any of his books in the stores. The last royalty check he received, in fact, was for only $13.13—for sales of about forty copies (most of which he himself bought).

Fitzgerald was certainly aware of his plummeting status; near the end of his life, writes author Garrison Keillor, "as far as Scott could see, he was a famous American failure . . . scorned and pitied for having squandered his gifts."[2] Fitzgerald suffered serious bouts of depression late in life, making it almost impossible for him to

write. In an autobiographical article in *Esquire* magazine late in his life, he compared himself to a "cracked plate":

> Sometimes, though, the cracked plate has to be retained in the pantry, has to be kept in service as a household necessity. It can never be warmed on the stove nor shuffled with the other plates in the dishpan; it will not be brought out for company but it will do to hold crackers late at night, or to go into the ice-box with the leftovers.[3]

A Dreary Funeral

Fitzgerald's funeral certainly reflected the mood of the last few years of his life. Historians note that in his original will—written when he was enjoying popularity and acclaim—he had specified a grand funeral, perhaps envisioning lots of flowers, music, and a lavish reception afterward for the hundreds of mourners. Five weeks before he died, however, he crossed out his original request. Instead of "grand," "cheap" was what he wanted.

The occasion was dreary and sad; the overcast skies gave way to rain by the time the funeral started. The funeral home, in a seedy, disreputable neighborhood in downtown Los Angeles, did a poor job in preparing his body for viewing; the cosmetic mortician used too much rouge on his cheeks. As one guest noted, "He was laid out to look like a cross between a floorwalker and a wax dummy. . . . But in technicolor."[4]

Few people attended the funeral. "Except for one bouquet of flowers and a few empty chairs," observed one witness, "there was nothing to keep him company except his casket. . . . I never saw a sadder [scene]."[5]

Fitzgerald had requested that he be buried beside his mother and father in the family plot in Rockville, Maryland. However, Catholic officials in Rockville would not permit it; he had not been a practicing Catholic at the time of his death. He was buried instead in Rockville Union Cemetery, two miles away.

Nothing Kind to Say

The lack of interest in Fitzgerald was apparent, too, by the obituaries in the newspapers. He was treated as a failed writer, a man whose talent had fled. Some editors predicted Fitzgerald's work would simply be forgotten. The *New York Times*, which had loved his work in the 1920s, called him "a real talent which never fully bloomed."[6]

F. Scott Fitzgerald's grave is located in Rockville, Maryland. Although considered one of America's best-loved writers, Fitzgerald died penniless and without recognition for his talents.

Other obituaries criticized Fitzgerald for the wild time period about which he wrote, disapprovingly citing "the penthouses, the long weekend drunks, the young people who were always on the brink of madness, the vacuous conversation, the lush intoxication of easy money."[7]

One of the most unkind notices of all was in New York's *Herald-Telegram,* which also ridiculed the author:

> The death of Scott Fitzgerald recalls memories of a queer brand of undisciplined and self-indulgent brats who were determined not to pull their weight in the boat and wanted the world to drop everything and sit down and bawl with them. A kick in the pants and a clout over the scalp were more like their needing, but all of us were more or less goofy then, so they enjoyed a very tolerant public.[8]

"His Reputation Has Soared"

It is certain that few, if any, of these critics would have believed in a renewed interest in Fitzgerald's work. However, in the test of time, the writings of F. Scott Fitzgerald stand out as some of the best in modern American literature.

"He's undergone a real renaissance," says one expert in American fiction. "Fitzgerald was pretty much assigned to the trash heap by the time he died, but his reputation has soared, especially in the last twenty years. It's not just among scholars either—people are reading his books because they're *good!*"[9]

In 1994, on the ninety-eighth anniversary of Fitzgerald's birth, his hometown of St. Paul, Minnesota, celebrated by renaming one of the city's finest theaters the Fitzgerald. Hundreds of people marked the occasion with a parade (some wore fashions of the 1920s) and a marathon reading of one of Fitzgerald's most famous novels, *The Great Gatsby.* Two years later, a bronze statue of the author was unveiled in that city while people cheered and waved copies of his books.

How can a man be pitied and criticized at the time of his death but be highly respected a generation or more later? What sort of man was F. Scott Fitzgerald that his life and works have endured such a stark contrast of reactions? And how is the world a different place because of his having lived?

1 Minnesota Roots

He was known throughout his life as Scott, but he was christened Francis Scott Key Fitzgerald. He was born on September 24, 1896, in a rented apartment on Laurel Street in St. Paul, Minnesota. His mother, Mollie, was terribly proud that one of her husband's great-grandmother's cousins was *the* Francis Scott Key, composer of "The Star Spangled Banner," and it was she who insisted on the name for her son.

The Fitzgerald Branch of the Family Tree

Edward Fitzgerald, Scott's father, was a gentle, well-mannered, elegantly dressed man. He loved to read, especially the romantic poetry of Byron and Poe, and collect trivia by browsing through the *Encyclopaedia Britannica.*

Edward was originally from Rockville, Maryland; his family was an old, established one, having been in America since the seventeenth century. These Fitzgeralds had been southern sympathizers during the Civil War. As a boy Edward had once rowed a Confederate spy across the Rockville River, and he could remember sitting atop a fence early one morning and watching General Jubal Early's battalions march toward Washington in an attempt to take over the capital. Years later, his son remembered these tales as an enchanting part of his boyhood.

Three-year-old F. Scott Fitzgerald is pictured with his father in a Christmas photo taken in 1899.

Edward attended Georgetown University for a while, but he never graduated. Instead, he decided to travel west to seek his fortune—first to Chicago and then to St. Paul, where he started the American Rattan and Wicker Works, a furniture manufacturing company.

Eccentric Mollie McQuillan

It was in St. Paul that Edward met twenty-seven-year-old Mollie McQuillan, the oldest child of Philip Francis McQuillan, an Irish immigrant whose wholesale grocery business in St. Paul had made him an enormously wealthy man by the time he died at age forty-four.

Mollie and her family lived on Summit Avenue, a lovely old residential street in the city. She was not beautiful by any standards; somewhat broad for her short stature, she had sallow skin and dark patches under her eyes. One relative privately called her "the most awkward and the homeliest woman I ever saw." [10]

Her behavior, too, was considered eccentric and odd by neighbors and relatives. She is said to have carried an umbrella even on the sunniest of days and to have frequently worn two mismatched shoes of different colors. Mollie also had a way of blurting out inappropriate or rude comments, without realizing how hurtful they could be. She once stared fixedly at a woman whose husband was ill. When asked why she was looking so intently, Mollie told

Fitzgerald's mother, Mollie McQuillan, lived on the fashionable and upper-class street of Summit Avenue in St. Paul, Minnesota.

the woman that she was trying to decide how she would look when she was in mourning.

The Loss of Two Sisters

They perhaps seemed an unlikely pair, but Edward and Mollie were married in 1890. It was believed that she had "persuaded" him to propose by threatening to throw herself off a bridge into the Mississippi River had he not. Perhaps, says one biographer, Edward's "beautiful Southern manners . . . left him defenseless before the determined attack." [11]

Mollie and Edward had two blond, blue-eyed daughters, and their life seemed relatively happy until 1896. While she was pregnant with her third child, the two little girls, ages one and three, died in an influenza epidemic. The sudden loss of their daughters devastated both parents. In a letter to his mother, Edward confessed, "I wonder sometimes if I will ever have any interest in life again; perhaps so, but certainly the keen zest of enjoyment is gone forever." [12]

Much later, Scott explained that his father was the one who was able to rally for his son's sake. "I was born several months after the death of my two elder sisters and [my father] felt what the effect of this would be on my mother, that he would be my only guide. He became that to the best of his ability." [13]

Overprotected and Spoiled

Despite his hefty ten-pound birth weight, Scott was a sickly baby, prone to colds and

Two-year-old Fitzgerald sits astride a hobbyhorse. The death of Scott's sisters before he was born deeply affected his parents, causing them to pamper and overprotect the boy.

bouts of pneumonia. His mother, having lost another baby in 1900 who lived only an hour, was understandably nervous about her son's health and overprotective of him.

When he was two, his mother took him to a health resort; she worried that his chronic wheezing and coughing would turn into pneumonia—or even tuberculosis. Fearing he might catch a chill, Mollie routinely bundled the boy in layer upon layer of clothing, so it was difficult for him to walk.

When the boy did become ill, he often had tantrums and steadfastly refused to take medicine, while his mother stood by helplessly. Dr. M. R. Ramsey, the Fitzgerald family doctor, recalled later how pampered and coddled young Scott was. "He was a very difficult and temperamental patient and refused to accept any regime which was not to his liking. This attitude he preserved throughout life."[14]

Scott's temper tantrums aside, both Mollie and Edward Fitzgerald were proud of their blond, blue-eyed son. Scott had a little cane and a silk coat like his father's, and on summer days Edward would walk downtown with his young son to get their shoes shined at the nearby hotel. His mother enjoyed showing off her son, too. At family gatherings or when visitors had come to call, she frequently had him recite poems he'd memorized or sing popular songs.

It was almost impossible for Mollie to punish her darling son, a fact that years later Scott regretted, for he thought she'd let him get away with far too much as a youngster. On the rare occasions when she did scold him, Scott recalled later, she lovingly referred to him as "a bad brownie." Later, Scott wrote to his own daughter about what a mistake it had been for his mother to let him have his way all the time. "I didn't know till 15," he admitted, "that there was anyone in the world except me. And it cost me *plenty*."[15]

Being Ashamed

By the time he was old enough to be in school, Scott had become somewhat embarrassed by his mother—not only for her pampering, coddling ways but for her eccentric behavior, which he was now old enough to recognize. In later essays he remembered her peculiar behavior and her disinterest in grooming. He recalled her going in for a manicure for just her right hand—because she could do the left herself. He had heard a family friend describe her as "dressed like the devil, always coming apart."[16]

His embarrassment is evident in a letter he sent his mother from camp when he was nine. He had written to his parents, feeling a little homesick and complaining of being picked on by a group of boys at the camp. Mollie wrote him back, telling Scott that she would come visit the camp and straighten the matter out for him. His reply discouraged her from coming:

> I received your letter this morning, and though I would like very much to have you up here I don't think you would like it as you know no one here except Mrs. Upton and she is busy most of the time. I don't think you would like the accommodations, as it is only a small town and no good hotels. There are some very nice boarding houses but about the only fare is lamb and beef.[17]

Dead Cats and Birthday Candles

Scott's childhood was not one of permanence; the family moved quite often, beginning in 1898. Edward's furniture manufacturing company had been struggling, but in that year, he finally had to close it down completely. With no capital to invest in a new business, he was forced to move his family to Buffalo, New York, where he would take a job as a traveling salesman for Procter and Gamble. Over the next decade they moved from Buffalo, to Syracuse, and back to Buffalo again.

There were some good memories, such as times spent with relatives from his father's side of the family. But there were some painful memories, as well. He remembered being six years old and terrified of a dead cat he saw in a nearby alley. He remembered a boy named Jack Butler hitting him in the forehead with a baseball bat.

He recalled, too, his seventh birthday party—to which no one came. He had sent out a dozen invitations to children in the Buffalo neighborhood in which they lived; however, heavy rains kept the children at home. Scott cried so hard that his mother allowed him to eat his entire birthday cake by himself—including the candles. Scott loved the taste of tallow until he was in his teens.

An Interest in Writing

Between being pampered and coddled by his mother as a youngster and moving so often, Scott had difficulty making friends.

A Fourth of July Thrashing

In her book The Real F. Scott Fitzgerald: Thirty-Five Years Later, *Sheila Graham recalls her conversations with the author about the kind of discipline he received when he was a child, and how his parenting style was different from that of his own parents.*

"Scott always liked his father, who, despite his failure in business, maintained a certain moral authority in the family. Scott remembered that it was the cultivated father, and not the energetic mother, who, when discipline had to be applied to him, did the thrashing.

The worst beating came after Scott, age six, wandered away from home on the Fourth of July and spent the day with a friend in a pear tree, oblivious that time was passing. The police were called in, the parents were frantic, and Scott watched the fireworks that evening with his pants still down and his behind smarting from the thrashing that had greeted his return.

Scott was, himself, to suffer the anxiety of the parent the time he telephoned from California to chat with Scottie at Vassar and discovered that she wasn't there. Scott was terribly disturbed, our weekend was ruined, and of course his daughter was all the time safely, happily with her friend . . . in Baltimore. Scottie was not physically beaten. Her punishment was worse—a halving of her $30 a month allowance. I received piteous letters from her, imploring me to intercede with her stern parent, which I did."

A photograph of Main Street in Buffalo, New York, taken around the time that the Fitzgeralds moved there in 1900. Edward Fitzgerald worked as a salesperson in the busy metropolis.

He was picked on frequently, both in and out of school. He was not very good at games or sports, he was bossy and critical of others, and he often lied to get attention.

For instance, when he was nine, he felt that he could not possibly be the true son of Mollie and Edward; he "just knew" he was someone far more important. He boasted to others in the neighborhood that he wasn't really a Fitzgerald but rather a foundling—a baby who had been left on the doorstep tagged with the royal name of Stuart. As one would expect, such statements did nothing to endear him to his peers.

As a result, he frequently found himself alone and learned to do more solitary things. One activity he realized that he had a talent for at quite a young age was writing. While he was often ill at ease around other people, in his writing he could make himself the center of the stories he created. Writing gave him power.

Scott wrote a school essay on George Washington and Ignatius Loyola, which

Early Reading

In his unpublished first novel, The Romantic Egotist, *Fitzgerald explains the great impression his reading as a child had on him. This excerpt from that novel is included in* Some Sort of Epic Grandeur: The Life of F. Scott Fitzgerald.

"First there was a book that was I think one of the big sensations of my life. It was nothing but a nursery book, but it filled me with the saddest and most yearning emotion. I have never been able to trace it since. It was about a fight that the large animals, like the elephant, had with the small animals, like the fox. The small animals won the first battle; but the elephants and the lions and tigers finally overcame them. The author was prejudiced in favor of the large animals, but my sentiment was all with the small ones. I wonder if even then I had a sense of the wearing-down power of big, respectable people. I can almost weep now when I think of that poor fox, the leader—the fox has somehow typified innocence to me ever since."

Scott Fitzgerald in 1906 at age ten. The young Fitzgerald loved to read.

earned high praise from his fourth grade teacher. He wrote a detective story about a necklace that was hidden under a secret door and a play based on events during the American Revolution. He also began keeping a "character book," a sort of jour-

Advice to a Younger Sister

Scott and his sister, Annabel, were never close; she was five years younger than he, and they had no interests in common. Nevertheless, when she became a teenager, he could not resist sending a letter advising her on the best ways to become popular with boys. The following excerpt is included in The Correspondence of F. Scott Fitzgerald, *edited by Matthew Bruccoli and Margaret Duggan.*

"Conversation, like grace, is a cultivated art. Only to the very few does it come naturally. You are, as you know, not a good conversationalist and you might very naturally ask, 'What do boys like to talk about?'

Boys like to talk about themselves—much more than girls. A girl named Helen Walcott once told me (and she was the most popular debutante in Washington one winter) that as soon as she got a man talking about himself she had him cinched and harnessed—they give themselves away. Here are some leading questions for a girl to use.

a) You dance so much better than you did last year.
b) How about giving me that sporty necktie when you're through with it.
c) You've got the longest eyelashes! (This will embarrass him, but he likes it.)
d) I hear you've got a 'line.'
e) Well, who's your latest crush?

Avoid

a) When do you go back to school?
b) How long have you been home?
c) It's warm, or the orchestra's good, or the floor's good.

Also avoid any talk about relations or mutual friends. . . . Don't be afraid of slang—use it, but be careful to use the most modern and sportiest. . . . Never talk to a boy about his school or college unless he starts the subject. . . .

As you get a little older you'll find that boys like to talk about such things as smoking and drinking. Always be very liberal—boys hate a prig—tell them you don't object to a girl smoking but don't like cigarettes yourself."

nal in which he wrote about his impressions of the other children in his class.

"Don't Let Us Go to the Poorhouse"

There is probably no incident that had more of an impact on Scott when he was young than when, in March 1908, his father was fired from his sales job in Buffalo. In an interview given in 1935, Fitzgerald recalls the day vividly:

> One afternoon—I was ten or eleven—the phone rang and my mother answered it. I didn't understand what she said but I felt that disaster had come to us. My mother, a little while before, had given me a quarter to go swimming. I gave the money back to her. I knew something terrible had happened and I thought she could not spare the money now.

Then I began to pray, "Dear God," I prayed, "please don't let us go to the poorhouse; please don't let us go to the poorhouse." A little while later my father came home. I had been right. He had lost his job.[18]

That afternoon was an important one for Scott, for it made him see his father in a completely different light. As Scott later wrote, "That morning he had gone out a comparatively young man, a man full of strength, full of confidence. He came home that evening an old man, a completely broken man. He had lost his essential drive, his immaculateness of purpose. He was a failure the rest of his days."[19]

The family would move back to St. Paul, to the security of Mollie's family's money. At age twelve, Scott was certainly aware of the loss of face they had suffered, a feeling that would stay with him—no matter how successful he became—for the rest of his life.

2 The Seeds of a Writing Life

The Fitzgeralds moved back to St. Paul in July 1908. While his mother and father lived nearby in the spare room of a friend's apartment, Scott and his younger sister, Annabel (who was born in 1901), lived for a time with their Grandmother McQuillan on Summit Avenue. Edward could not yet afford a large enough residence for the whole family.

"If It Weren't for Your Grandfather McQuillan"

Mollie was able to get Edward a job as a wholesale grocer in the family business, but he seemed listless and unenthusiastic about it. He kept up appearances and pretended to be in business—he kept samples of coffee, rice, and dried fruit in a rolltop desk in the corner of his brother-in-law's real estate office—but he made no real effort to do much selling.

When he needed supplies, such as postage stamps, he merely charged them to his wife's account. Edward, at fifty-five years old, was not interested in working very hard, especially when there seemed to be plenty of McQuillan money to support the family.

His lack of ambition was pointed out time and again by Mollie, who used her share of the McQuillan fortune to support her family. She was fond of pointing out that fact; she frequently asked the children the rhetorical question, "If it weren't for your Grandfather McQuillan, where would we be now?"[20]

The Class System of St. Paul

Such tension was not lost on young Scott, who was quickly becoming aware of the difference between his family and the others in his St. Paul neighborhood. The St. Paul of the early 1900s was increasingly status-conscious; historians referred to the city then as "the Boston of the Middle West." It was the age of tycoons who had made their fortunes in fur trading, wholesaling, journalism, and real estate. It was the home of railroader James J. Hill, lumberman E. L. Hersey, and publisher Charles Ames. St. Paul—at least the Summit Avenue portion—was money, rank, and tradition.

As Scott compared his own family with the families who lived all around him, he understood more and more that he was something of an outsider. Although his mother's family had money, they were merchants—far down on the social ladder. And although his father's family of Maryland had title, his father's failure at business made that title almost worthless. Much later in life, he wrote to fellow author John O'Hara and described the shame he felt because of it all:

> I am half black Irish and half old American stock with the usual exaggerated ancestral pretensions. The black Irish half of the family had the money and looked down upon the Maryland side of the family who had, and really had, that series of reticences and obligations that go under the poor old shattered word "breeding.". . . So being born in that atmosphere of crack, wise crack and countercrack I developed a two-cylinder inferiority complex.[21]

Scott was both fascinated and angry with the social system that kept him on the fringe of the wealthy class of St. Paul. The anger was slow to cool; even as an adult he

The Fitzgeralds returned to St. Paul, Minnesota, in 1908 to be near Mollie Fitzgerald's family. Scott Fitzgerald noticed the difference between his family's relative poverty and his neighbors' wealth.

admitted, "I have never been able to forgive the rich for being rich, and it has colored my entire life and works." [22]

Less of an Outcast

Scott found a much more interesting social life when his family moved back to St. Paul in 1908. Because of living with his grandmother on Summit Avenue for a time, he had a large and active group of children with whom to play. It is interesting that, although Scott was not as well liked as many of the other children, he was not a loner. His need for recognition required an audience, after all.

His companions were children of the well-to-do families of St. Paul, and they participated in a busy social life. Winters were spent in bobsledding or skiing parties; in the summers many of the children went to summer homes on White Bear Lake, just north of St. Paul. Scott was sometimes invited to visit for a few days, which meant he got to ride out on the trolley from St. Paul—something he really enjoyed.

Looking back on this time in his life, he had fond memories of the houses of several of his playmates. His friend Cecil Read had an attic where several of the boys spent time on rainy afternoons. One of the most popular of their activities was forming secret clubs, of which Scott almost always declared himself president.

Betty Ames and her brother Ted were childhood friends whose backyard, Fitzgerald later remembered, was the perfect place for young teens to gather in the afternoons. He used the Ameses' yard in a story he wrote in 1928 called "The Scandal Detectives":

It had many advantages. It was large, open to other yards on both sides, and it could be entered upon skates or bicycles from the street. It contained an old seesaw, a swing, and a pair of flying rings; but it had been a rendezvous before these were put up, for it had a child's quality—the thing that makes young people huddle inextricably on uncomfortable steps and desert the houses of their friends to herd on the obscure premises of "people nobody knows.". . . There were deep shadows there all day long and ever something vague in bloom, and patient dogs around, and brown spots worn bare by countless circling wheels and dragging feet. [23]

St. Paul Academy

Beginning in 1909, twelve-year-old Scott was enrolled in St. Paul Academy, a private boys' school just a few blocks from his grandmother's house. The student body was composed of forty boys between the ages of ten and eighteen—many of them the sons of St. Paul's elite.

Although an extremely bright, verbal boy, Scott was not much of a student. He recalled later that he spent time writing when he should have been listening instead. "I wrote all through every class in school," he admits, "in the back of my geography book and the first year Latin and in the margin of themes and declensions and mathematics problems." [24]

He was not popular with the other boys—not because his grades were mediocre but because he tended to be more conceited than the other children. He was known as the "freshest" boy in school, the one with the sharp tongue, the one who always had a witty but critical remark about everyone he met. Fitzgerald later remembered that it was at St. Paul Academy that he "endured the humiliation of seeing the school paper, the St. Paul Academy *Now and Then,* print in 1909: 'If anyone can poison Scotty or stop his mouth in some way, the school at large and myself will be obliged.'"[25]

"I Read My Story Through at Least Six Times"

It was during this time he began to think of himself as a writer. His first published story, "The Mystery of the Raymond Mortgage," was printed in the October 1909 issue of *Now and Then.*

When he found out his submission had been accepted for the paper, Scott was ecstatic. So impatient was he for the issue to come out, in fact, that he hung around the printer's office until he was finally told he had to leave because he was being a nuisance. When the papers were delivered to the classroom one afternoon, he was so excited that he bounced up and down in his seat.

He later recalled how proud he was when he held the paper and saw his name in print for the first time. "I read my story through at least six times," he admitted, "and all day I loitered in the corridors and counted the number of [students and teachers] who were reading it, and tried to ask people casually if they had read it."[26]

That detective story was followed early in 1910 by a sports story called "Reade, Substitute Right Half," about a small, thin boy who comes off the bench to win an important football game for his school. A third, called "A Debt of Honor," based on some of his father's stories about the Civil War, was about a Confederate soldier who falls asleep on sentry duty and must compensate by performing a heroic act shortly thereafter.

A Passion for the Theater

Besides writing short stories, Scott had an even bigger interest, one that gave him a great deal more satisfaction—the theater. Since he was a small child, he had loved fantasizing that he was a heroic character from one of the books he was reading or from a play he had seen. After seeing a play about the Revolutionary War one afternoon, seven-year-old Scott came home, wrapped himself in a red scarf, and acted out the part of the hero of the play, Paul Revere.

Scott loved going to the Orpheum Theater in downtown St. Paul to watch the Saturday vaudeville shows and operettas. He was not content merely to be a spectator, however. Having an uncanny ability to remember things after hearing them only once, he often mimicked entire scenes from the plays he saw for his family and friends—sometimes reciting long, dramatic speeches completely by memory.

It was during his years at St. Paul Academy that Scott began writing plays. He was especially interested in being a part of the Elizabethan drama club, named after its sponsor and drama coach, twenty-year-old Elizabeth Magoffin. She was enthusiastic about Scott's work and allowed his first play, *The Girl from Lazy J,* to be performed in her home on Summit Avenue.

"The Mystery of the Raymond Mortgage"

Fitzgerald's first appearance in print was in the St. Paul Academy school magazine when he was thirteen. This excerpt, from Matthew Bruccoli's Some Sort of Epic Grandeur, *is compelling and readable, even though it is undoubtedly juvenile.*

"'Up the stairs,' shouted Syrel, and we followed him, taking two steps at a bound. As we reached the top landing, we were met by a young man.

'What right have you to enter this house?' he demanded.

'The right of the law,' replied Syrel.

'I didn't do it,' broke out the young man. 'It was this way. Agnes Raymond loved me—she did not love Standish—he shot her; and God did not let her murder go unrevenged. It was well Mrs. Raymond killed him, for his blood would have been on my hands. I went back to see Agnes before she was buried. A man came in. I knocked him down. I didn't know until a moment ago that Mrs. Raymond had killed him.'

'I forgot Mrs. Raymond!' screamed Syrel. 'Where is she?'

'She is out of your power forever,' said the young man.

Syrel brushed past him and, with Smidy and I following, burst open the door of the room at the head of the stairs. We rushed in.

On the floor lay a woman, and as soon as I touched her heart, I knew she was beyond the doctor's skill.

'She has taken poison,' I said. Syrel looked around; the young man had gone. And we stood there aghast in the presence of death."

Even though one of his best friends, Tubby Washington, infuriated the playwright by not reading his lines properly, the play was a success, and Scott wrote several more, many of which he also starred in and directed.

Miss Magoffin was very impressed with the speed and ease with which the boy rewrote lines or made other changes in his scripts. "When it came to rewriting," she once recalled, "Fitzgerald was indefatigable, retiring to a corner and tossing off new lines with his ever-facile pen." [27]

Dancing Class

Learning to dance was another activity that occupied Scott's time during his St. Paul Academy days. The lessons were held on Grand Avenue—above Ramaley's catering service, delicatessen, and bakery—in a pink-and-white ballroom known as Ramaley Hall. Starting in 1902, the hall had been home to the dancing school, headed by Professor William H. Baker, a roly-poly, apple-shaped man with a white mustache who was amazingly light on his feet.

In addition to teaching boys and girls to dance, Professor Baker moonlighted as a bartender at the White Bear Yacht Club several nights a week. The fact that the professor was one of his own best customers was no secret, for his pupils could frequently smell alcohol on his breath.

Scott's mother, Mollie, was delighted that he was a part of the class, which was known as the "Grand Avenue Gentry," since

Even at age eleven, Scott Fitzgerald showed a talent for writing. He was also one of the few boys to excel at a weekly dance class.

most of the forty boys and girls were from St. Paul's elite families. It signified that a Fitzgerald was making inroads into the upper class, even though Edward Fitzgerald was understood to be something of a failure at business.

"The Dancing Lessons . . . Completely Ruined Our Saturdays"

There was a vast difference in attitudes about the class, and it usually fell along gender lines. The girls looked forward to the Saturday classes, remembers one participant, for they got to wear party dresses and special soft dancing slippers. One girl, a playmate of Scott's named Betty Ames, loved Professor Baker's school so much that she begged her parents to postpone a European vacation for three weeks so she didn't miss a single lesson.

In addition to dressing up for the lessons, the girls also enjoyed watching the boys struggle uncomfortably in clothes they didn't like—serge suits, knickers, Windsor ties, black patent leather shoes, white cotton gloves, and high starched collars of the variety worn by highbred English boys. Most of the boys hated the classes, attending only because their parents forced them. To them, it was an unwelcome interruption of their weekend. Recalls one classmate of Scott's, "The dancing lessons lasted all of Saturday afternoons and completely ruined our Saturdays. After going to school all week, the only day we had to ourselves was Saturday, and it had to be wasted learning the Grand March."[28]

Interestingly, however, Scott didn't mind having his weekend interrupted. He was an enthusiastic student and, as a result, was much favored by Professor Baker. Most of the girls rated him as an excellent dance partner, too. Since that was the only time in his life he had dance instruction, he must have learned well: Years later, his future wife, Zelda, was so swept off her feet by Scott's dancing that she wrote, "There seemed to be some heavenly support beneath his shoulder blades . . . as if he secretly enjoyed the ability to fly but was walking as a compromise to convention."[29]

Girlfriends

While many of his twelve- and thirteen-year-old peers were reluctant to have girlfriends, Scott was quite eager. He found girls interesting—and had since he was nine or ten years old, when he lived in Buffalo. There he met a girl named Kitty Williams, the first love of his life.

Scott was infatuated with Kitty, even more so because she didn't feel the same way about him right away.

I met her first at dancing school, and as Mr. van Arnam [the dancing teacher] chose me to lead the march; I asked her to be my partner. The next day she told Marie Louty and Marie repeated it to Dorothy Knox who in turn passed it on to Earl, that I was third in her affections. . . . I then and there resolved that I should gain first place.[30]

During his early teens in St. Paul, Scott was even more eager to win the hearts of the prettiest, most charming girls in his circle of friends. In 1910 and 1911 he kept a journal entitled *Thoughtbook of Francis Scott*

A Childhood Romance

One of Scott's first crushes was Kitty Williams, a young girl he had met when living in Buffalo. In his book Invented Lives: F. Scott and Zelda Fitzgerald, *James R. Mellow includes an excerpt from Scott's diary during this youthful romance, detailing how he ranked among the other boys who liked Kitty.*

"I don't remember who was first, but I know that Earl was second, and as I was already quite overcome by her charms I then and there resolved that I would gain first place. . . . Finally she asked me if I was going to Robin's party and it was there my eventful day was. We played post office, pillow, clap in and clap out, and other foolish but interesting games. It was impossible for me to count the number of times I kissed Kitty that afternoon. At any rate, when we went home I had secured the coveted first place. I held this until dancing school stopped in the spring and then relinquished it to Johnny Gowns, a rival. On Valentine's Day that year Kitty received no less than eighty-four valentines."

Key Fitzgerald, in which he chronicled his relationships with various girls and kept a running log of his attempts to be popular in school. The *Thoughtbook* was kept secret, in a metal box under his bed.

Flirting by Signs

One of the girls he wrote about in his *Thoughtbook* was Violet Stockton, a dark-haired southern girl who was visiting her aunt in St. Paul for the summer. It is Violet whose name occupies most of the *Thoughtbook;* he fell completely in love with her. He tried to be amusing and clever, and for her entertainment he developed a game called "Indians," in which the neighborhood children had make-believe wars with croquet mallets for guns.

Scott was not the only one that summer who was entranced with Violet; his two friends Jack Mitchell and Arthur Foley were also in love with her. Throughout that summer, according to his *Thoughtbook,* the boys tried various ways to win her heart. Arthur and Jack sneaked up behind her and snipped off tiny locks of her hair. That made Violet angry, so Scott decided to try something less childish.

Violet had let her friends know that she found Scott to be both attractive and very polite. She also told one friend that she thought Scott's teeth were so white and even that she wished they were hers. However, she also let it be known that she felt Scott acted a bit superior to everyone else.

Violet herself had a journal, which she called *Flirting by Signs.* Scott and Jack, attempting to read what she had written about them, managed to steal the book.

Enraged, Violet went into her aunt's house and slammed the door. Scott, too, got mad and went home, as he wrote that evening in his *Thoughtbook:*

> Immediately, Violet repented and called me up on the phone to see if I was mad. However, I did not want to make up just then and so I slammed down the receiver. The next morning I went down to Jack's to find that Violet had said that she was not coming out that day. It was now my turn to repent and I did so and she came out that evening.[31]

The two made up, and Violet even gave him a box of candy on his birthday—although she did give her ring to Arthur Foley as a remembrance and asked him to send his photograph.

Heading East

In the spring of 1911, Scott's parents decided he should leave St. Paul Academy. His grades were not good, and it seemed he needed a much stricter atmosphere if he was to do well in school. They decided he would go to a boarding school in the fall.

The chosen school was the Newman Academy, a Catholic prep school in Hackensack, New Jersey, less than an hour away from New York City. The academy had been started in 1890 by a cardinal from Baltimore as a way of providing a high-class, New England prep school education to the sons of wealthy Catholic families. The Fitzgeralds hoped that at Newman Scott would settle down to studying more diligently and, as a result, have a better chance

The Most Unpopular Boy at School

At fifteen, F. Scott Fitzgerald attended Newman Academy in New Jersey. In spite of his enthusiasm for the school, Fitzgerald had a hard time making friends and was generally disliked.

of being admitted to a good college. For these reasons, the $850 per year tuition was felt to be a sound investment.

Far from being resentful at being sent east, Scott was ecstatic. For years he had enjoyed reading books about boys at eastern prep schools and had always envisioned himself there, taking part in football games and having fun with friends. Years later in a story called "The Freshest Boy," Fitzgerald's descriptions of the hero's feelings of entering such a prep school are autobiographical: "He had lived with such intensity on so many stories of boarding-school life that, far from being homesick, he had a glad feeling of recognition and familiarity."[32]

The reality, however, was far more grim. Scott had even less success at making friends at Newman than he had at St. Paul Academy. Within just a few weeks, Scott had become the most unpopular boy in the school. He was cocky and egotistical—irritating to the faculty as well as his fellow students.

He was, agree Scott's classmates at Newman, a misfit wanting so much to be popular that he seemed to be trying too hard. One recalled later that Scott was "eager to be liked by his companions and almost vain in seeking praise." Another said that "he was unpopular starting out at Newman partly because his good looks prompted classification as a sissy, which was reinforced by what appeared to be a lack of physical courage."[33]

The sadness of being so disliked was recorded, too—this time in his first novel, *This Side of Paradise.* "He went all wrong at the start," he writes of the hero, Amory, "was generally considered both conceited and arrogant, and universally detested. . . . He was unbearably lonely, desperately unhappy. . . . Miserable, confined to bounds, unpopular with both faculty and students—that was Amory's first term."[34]

Failing at Football

One of the ways Scott tried to gain popularity was by playing football. As with so many of his other notions about "the way things should be," he was captivated by the idea of the football player saving the day for the school's honor, which was a common theme of the books he had read as a young teenager. Although slight of build and more than a little afraid of the ball, Scott went out for football at Newman.

The best he could do was the third team—"the scrubs," as they were called. He didn't care, however, for he usually got to see at least a few minutes of playing time in each game. In one important game against Newark Academy, however, he humiliated himself by running backward, away from an opposing player, to avoid the pain of being tackled. Both his teammates and the Newman fans along the sidelines were disgusted with him, and they taunted him unmercifully.

He wrote about the incident later, insisting that his actions were misunderstood:

> I remember the desolate ride in the bus back to the train and the desolate ride back to school with everybody

thinking I had been yellow on the occasion, when actually I was just distracted and sorry for that opposing end. That's the truth. I've been afraid plenty of times but that wasn't one of the times.[35]

"A Back-Door Way Out of Facing Reality"

Bitter about the way he was being cast as a coward, Scott wrote a thirty-six-line poem entitled "Football" about an exciting moment in a prep school game. He submitted it to the school paper, the *Newman News,* and found that he gained a little respect because of it. In addition, the poem greatly pleased his father, who loved the ringing, descriptive tone:

> Good he's free; no, see that halfback
> Gaining up behind him slow.

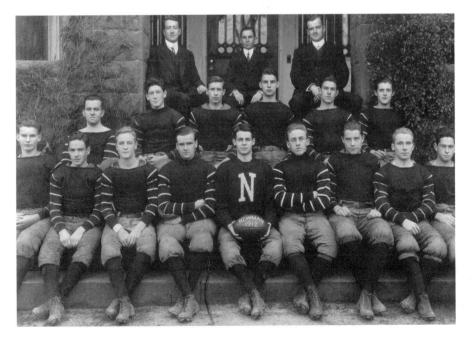

F. Scott Fitzgerald (front row, third from left) poses with the Newman Academy football team.

Crash! they're down; he threw him
    nicely,—
Classy tackle, hard and low.[36]

In writing the poem, Scott said later, it "made me as big a hit with my father as if I had become a football hero. So when I went home that Christmas vacation it was in my mind that if you weren't able to function in action, you might at least be able to tell about it, because you felt the same intensity. It was a back-door way out of facing reality."[37]

Solace in the Theater

The theater, like the time he spent writing, was one of the few pleasures Scott enjoyed at Newman. The school's proximity to New York City made it easy for him to visit for an evening and see the stars of the stage. He saw George M. Cohan in *The Little Millionaire,* Ina Clair in *The Quaker Girl,* and Gertrude Bryan in *Little Boy Blue*—three Broadway hits of 1911.

After seeing firsthand the excitement well-done theater generated among its audiences, Scott resolved to become a serious playwright. Riding the train from Hackensack back to St. Paul for summer vacation, he began writing a play, *The Captured Shadow,* which Elizabeth Magoffin would love and which would be performed later that summer by the Elizabethan drama club.

However, his grades for the first year were more than disappointing. He had failed algebra, French, physics, and a class on Caesar; his grades for English and Latin were almost as bad. Clearly, Newman Academy was not working out as well as his family had hoped.

Father Fay

He returned to Newman for his senior year with a determination to do better. He continued to play with the football team and actually got a compliment in a story in the school paper, which commended him for "fine running with the ball." (Some biographers have noted that this story might actually have been written by Fitzgerald himself.)

Fitzgerald had little patience with classes that did not interest him, attaining poor grades in all subjects. He preferred attending the theater to studying.

A Distinct Style

By the time Fitzgerald was fifteen or sixteen, his writing had acquired a distinct style—especially the skillful use of description. The following excerpt from his 1912 story, "The Trail of the Duke," is included in Matthew Bruccoli's Some Sort of Epic Grandeur: The Life of F. Scott Fitzgerald.

"It was a hot July night. Inside, through screen, window, and door fled the bugs and gathered around the lights like so many humans at a carnival, buzzing, thugging, whirring. From out the night into the houses came the sweltering late summer heat, overpowering and enervating, bursting against the walls and enveloping all mankind like a huge smothering blanket. In the drug stores the clerks, tired and grumbling, handed out ice cream to hundreds of thirsty but misled civilians, while in the corners buzzed the electric fans in a whirring mockery of coolness. In the flats that line upper New York, pianos (sweating ebony perspiration) ground out ragtime tunes of last winter and here and there a wan woman sang the air in a hot soprano. In the tenements, shirt-sleeves gleamed like beacon lights in steady rows along the streets in tiers of from four to eight according to the number of stories in the house. In a word, it was a typical, hot New York summer night."

He published three stories in the school paper that year: "A Luckless Santa Claus," "Pain and the Scientist," and "The Trail of the Duke," which literary experts say foreshadowed his great talent in characterization and description. Scott's grades, unfortunately, did not show the same promise; as a result, he was not allowed as many free days off campus to enjoy the theater in New York.

Scott did make a good friend at Newman that year, however. He was Father Cyril Sigourney Webster Fay, a thirty-seven-year-old priest who was a trustee of Newman Academy. Fay certainly stood out in a crowd, according to one description:

The huge . . . priest, almost a pure albino, had a shrill, high-pitched, giggling voice. He was extremely near-sighted and enormously fat. His thin, pale yellow hair, rising above a broad forehead, was parted in the middle. A thick pince-nez distorted his pink, watery eyes. His pudge nose, round face, triple chins and thick neck emphasized his porcine appearance and made him look twenty years older than his actual age.[38]

Father Fay was interested in music, the theater, literature, and good conversation, and he became an important influence in Scott's life. He enjoyed reading whatever the boy was writing at the time; the two talked for hours about characters and plot. Father Fay also introduced Scott to his friends among the social and intellectual elite in Washington, including Shane Leslie, who would later recommend Scott's first novel to Scribner's (a large publishing house), and Henry Adams, a writer and historian. His new friendship with these men was able to compensate for the unhappiness he experienced at Newman, as well as give him a bit of confidence to tackle the next hurdle in his life—college.

Chapter

3 Away to Princeton

The question of where he would attend college had only one answer, according to Scott, and that was "Princeton." For as long as he could remember, the school represented everything that he wanted a college to be, and it was unthinkable to him that he would go anywhere else.

But his family had other ideas. Relatives on his father's side urged him to consider Georgetown, a good Catholic university. His mother begged him to apply to the University of Minnesota—the tuition was cheaper, and he could live at home. But he wasn't interested in either of those.

"I Think of All Harvard Men as Sissies"

There was something heroic about Princeton, especially in the way its football team played. During his first year at Newman Academy, he had watched a Princeton-Harvard game in which a Princeton player named Sam White blocked a kick and ran ninety-five yards for a touchdown. He saved his ticket stub for that game and pasted it in his scrapbook, with the caption, "Sam White decides me for Princeton."[39]

He liked the idea of Princeton, too, because of its appeal to class. The school had the reputation as an Ivy League college for Southerners; with his father's family's Maryland roots, he enjoyed the image of himself as a Southerner with an old, established family name. Princeton was a place where he'd truly belong.

In his mind, Princeton was far better than either Yale or Harvard—both of which had excellent academic reputations. "I don't know why," he wrote later, "but I think of all Harvard men as sissies, like I used to be, and all Yale men as wearing big blue sweaters and smoking pipes. . . . I think of Princeton as being lazy and good-looking and aristocratic."[40]

Another aspect of Princeton that he liked was its famed Triangle Club, a drama group that wrote and produced a musical each year that was performed during Christmas break in twelve large cities across the United States, including St. Louis, Baltimore, Chicago, and even New York. Nothing would please him more than to be a part of such performances.

Talking His Way In

There were two obstacles that made his attending Princeton unlikely. The first— money—was solved when Grandmother

Always status-conscious, Fitzgerald virtually talked his way into the prestigious and academically challenging Princeton University by promising to get better grades than he had in high school.

McQuillan died that summer. Mollie's share of the estate was $125,000, a fortune in those days. Because of his mother's inheritance, Scott could afford to attend any school that would accept him.

But that was precisely the problem. His grades, at both St. Paul Academy and Newman Academy, had been poor. He took his entrance exams during the summer of 1913, just before his seventeenth birthday, and was promptly turned down—even though he admittedly cheated on the exams.

The admissions committee asked him to retake the exams and to come in for a personal interview. Even this second time, he would have been turned down, except for some fast talking—he told the committee it wouldn't be right to deny him, espe-

cially on that day, his birthday. He quickly agreed to their conditions that he would get much better grades than he'd been getting and that he would retake the admissions test the following December. Elated, Scott sent his parents a hasty telegram instructing them to send his football pads and cleats immediately.

The Football Fanatic

As at Newman, football was the fastest way to becoming popular, or becoming a "big man on campus," as it was called then. Football was more of a "gentleman's sport" than it is today; it was usual for 140- and

150-pounders to play first string. The greatest athlete in Princeton history—and one of the most popular boys on campus—was a senior named Hobey Baker. At five foot nine and 167 pounds, playing without a helmet, Baker seemed to Scott the most heroic figure he'd ever seen.

At five foot six and 138 pounds, Scott lasted through only the first day of practice before being cut. Though he was disappointed, he continued to be a strong, enthusiastic supporter of Princeton football from the bleachers. Sometimes his enthusiasm was a bit too much for some of the coaches, who received detailed instructions from Scott about how they could improve their offense. Long after leaving college, Scott would call Princeton football coaches—sometimes in the middle of the night before a big game against Harvard or Yale—to recommend a particular play that he felt was sure to be successful.

Interestingly, it was the Princeton football team that occupied his last thoughts; he was making notes in the *Princeton Alumni Weekly* when he suffered his fatal heart attack. In his copy of the magazine, reports Fitzgerald historian Andre Le Vot, "a pencil line still runs wildly down the page of a story about the current football season." [41]

The Social Ladder

His failure to make the team was not as depressing as it could have been, for he was enjoying so many other aspects of Princeton. Especially in the first months, he was almost giddy with the realization that he had fulfilled his dream of being a Princeton man. He loved the campus, as it was steeped in tradition—having been founded two centuries before. Ten years after he left, he still saw it in the same way:

> Two tall spires and then suddenly all around you spreads out the loveliest riot of Gothic architecture in America, battlement linked to battlement, hall to hall, arch-broken, vine-covered, luxuriant and lovely over two square miles of green grass. Here is no monotony, no feeling that it was all built yesterday at the whim of last week's millionaire. [42]

With so much tradition surrounding him, Scott was aware that it was important to find a niche for himself. If he had thought St. Paul had a stratified society, then Princeton's was even more so.

Most of the young men at Princeton (it was an all-male college) came from upper-class feeder schools, and their families moved in the same social circles. Scott, on the other hand, had come from a relatively obscure Catholic prep school, and he felt—as he always had—that he hailed from the wrong side of the tracks. "That was always my experience," he wrote later, "a poor boy in a rich town; a poor boy in a rich boy's school; a poor boy in a rich man's club at Princeton." [43]

He had aspirations, however, without knowing exactly what they were. "I want to pull strings . . . or be Princetonian chairman or Triangle President," says Amory in Fitzgerald's first novel, *This Side of Paradise.* "I want to be admired." [44]

The Preceptorial System

Being admired for academic work was going to be a difficult challenge for Scott. His first term he had seven compulsory courses:

Latin, plane trigonometry, algebra, English literature, French, physics, and personal hygiene. In addition to these, he was required to take an eighth course in mathematics to prepare him for retaking the entrance examination in December.

Scott had never been much of a student, and things did not change much at Princeton. He had always found math and science dull, and he never had a knack for memorizing conjugations and declensions, so foreign languages were a mystery to him. He spent most of his energy on his English classes and was pleased that the department included Alfred Noyes, the poet who had written "The Highwayman."

But most of his teachers he found disappointing and uninteresting. Particularly unpleasant to him was the method of instruction at Princeton. Called the preceptorial system, it consisted of a lecture by a professor, followed by a small-group weekly meeting with a teaching assistant, or preceptor. The idea was that the preceptor would strengthen a student's understanding of the more impersonal lectures.

Fitzgerald, left, is pictured with two other boys during his freshman year at Princeton. The young man continued to pay little attention to his classes.

But Scott felt as though he were being cheated by having to attend the weekly preceptorial sessions. Instead of listening and taking notes, he wrote scathing attacks on the young precept, a man named Griffin:

Gee but this man Griffin is terrible. I sit here bored to death and hear him pick English poetry to pieces. Small man, small mind. Snotty, disagreeable. Damn him. "Neat" is his favorite word. Imagine Shakespeare being neat. Yesterday I counted and found that he used the expression "Isn't that so" fifty-four times. Oh, what a disagreeable silly ass he is. He's going to get married. God help his wife. Poor girl. She's in for a bad time. They say that Griffin has made more men leave the English department than any other preceptor in College. The slovenly old fool! *I have the most terrible preceptors!* [45]

Skating By

He rarely bothered to hide his disdain for his teachers. After being warned repeatedly about his tardiness to class, Scott refused to change his ways, and declared, "Sir—it's absurd to expect me to be on time. I'm a genius." [46] Although there is no record of his professor's reaction, one must assume Scott's attitude did not help his reputation among the staff. So low was their opinion of him, in fact, that one professor in the English department who went on to become chairman would not believe, years later, that Fitzgerald was the true author of *The Great Gatsby*.

It seems that the results of his exams for the first term did not help his reputa-tion either. The Princeton grading system did not use As and Bs; instead, a student was given a rank by group for each class. First group, for instance, was the highest standing. Second group was high; third group, satisfactory; fourth group, below average; fifth group, poor; sixth group, unsatisfactory; and seventh group, very unsatisfactory.

Scott's average was a 5.17 for the first term—barely passing. His highest mark was in English literature, but that was fourth group, below average. He failed trigonometry, hygiene, and algebra. And since it was school policy that any failed class had to be made up the following term, his poor performance ensured a harder curriculum the following term. It was, say biographers, a pattern he would keep up the whole time he remained at Princeton.

Ironically, he wrote later that it would have been tempting to cheat on exams but he regarded the honor system at Princeton a sacred tradition. (This from a young man who cheated his way into the college in the first place.) "I can think of a dozen times," he wrote, "when a page of notes glanced at in a washroom would have made the difference between failure and success for me, but I can't recall any moral struggles in the matter." [47]

Fie! Fie! Fi-Fi!

As at Newman Academy, his writing was an outlet for his ambitions to excel at something. Each year, the Triangle Club, which he had longed to participate in, had a competition for the best submitted script for the following year's musical. Scott had been working during the fall on a script

Fitzgerald (in hat) acts in his play The Coward *performed in 1913 at Princeton University. Eschewing class work, Fitzgerald devoted his time to writing and acting for the university's extracurricular Triangle Club.*

and was greatly pleased when Walker Ellis, a junior from New Orleans who was president of the Triangle Club, selected it as the winner.

Scott's script centered around an American con man who becomes the prime minister of Monaco and his wife, a hotel manicurist. It also included a subplot about the love affair between an Englishman and a flapper named Celeste. In the Princeton tradition, every role was played by a student—and since it was an all-male school, that included female roles. In fact, it was rumored that one of the reasons Ellis chose Fitzgerald's entry was because it had a part he himself wanted—the part of the manicurist. Scott chose to be Celeste and looked forward eagerly to the tour of *Fie! Fie! Fi-Fi!* the following Christmas vacation.

Two Good Friends

It was in his first year at Princeton that Scott made two good friends, something of a rare commodity in his life up until then. The first was John Peale Bishop, who although being in the same class as Scott was actually three years older; a boyhood bout of tuberculosis had delayed his school career. Bishop loved literature, and the first time he spoke with Scott, he spotted him as somewhat of a phony. "We talked about books," he said later, "those I had read, which were not many; those Fitzgerald had read, which were even less; those he said he had read, which were many, many more."[48]

Scott's exaggerated claims notwithstanding, Bishop proved to be a loyal and thoughtful lifelong friend. Scott valued the times they spent together, especially those discussing poetry. He found Bishop to be one of the only people he'd ever met—including the faculty at Princeton—who truly understood it. Much later, in a letter to his daughter, Scott tried to get his daughter to find someone with whom she could share poetry.

> It isn't something easy to get started on by yourself. You need, at the beginning, some enthusiast who also knows his way around—John Peale Bishop performed that office for me at Princeton. . . . He made me see . . . the difference between poetry and non-poetry. After that one of my first discoveries was that some of the professors who were teaching poetry really hated it and didn't know what it was about. I got in a series of endless scraps with them so that finally I dropped English altogether.[49]

His other good friend was Edmund "Bunny" Wilson, whom Scott later called "my intellectual conscience."[50] The son of a highly successful trial lawyer and once the New Jersey attorney general, Wilson was everything Scott was not. He had position and rank, he had money, he was a superb scholar. Even so, the two enjoyed each other, perhaps because they were worlds apart. There seemed to be an unspoken agreement between them that Wilson was the wise intellectual, while Scott was the eager young upstart.

It is interesting that both Wilson and Bishop went on to become well-known literary figures. Bishop wrote several novels and books of poetry while dealing with depression and poor health. Wilson wrote many books on scholarly subjects, including history, biblical studies, and literary criticism.

Disappointment—and Pride

Scott was tutored during the summer between his freshman and sophomore years, and he came back to Princeton early to take his makeup exam in geometry. Unfortunately, he failed the test. If that had meant that he had to retake a course or take another exam, it would not have been nearly as catastrophic for him. But this failure resulted in the Faculty Committee on Non-Athletic Organizations banning him from all extracurricular activities at Princeton—including his tour with *Fie! Fie! Fi-Fi!*

He was still able to work on the play, however, and that is what he devoted his time to doing. Walker Ellis, his collaborator on the play, somehow gave himself credit for the story, even though it had been Scott's script; Fitzgerald is listed only as the lyricist.

Scott had never before written song lyrics, and they were amazingly good. One of the most popular songs, "A Slave to Modern Improvements," has this chorus:

> A victim to modern improvements am I,
> I've a silver chest and a crystal eye;
> A platinum lung and a grafted nose,
> Aluminum fingers,
> Asbestos toes.
> And when I walk I clank and clash,
> And rust when damp, you see;
> And the wildest lot of anonymous trash
> That ever crossed the sea.[51]

From the moment the show began its tour (without him) in early December 1914, it got rave reviews. Ellis got much of the credit for "his" script, although Scott's lyrics were singled out for praise, too. The Baltimore *Sun* claimed that his lyrics were the best part of the show. A New York newspaper said that there were Broadway musicals that had "less vivacity, less sparkling humor and less genuine music." And one of Scott's favorite clippings was from the Louisville *Post,* which stated that he had a great future: "The lyrics of the songs were written by F. S. Fitzgerald, who could take his place right now with the brightest writers of witty lyrics in America."[52]

Meeting Ginevra

Resigned to going home to St. Paul for the Christmas holidays instead of on the exciting tour he'd envisioned, Scott busied himself writing a play for the Triangle Club for the following year. He and Edmund Wilson had decided to collaborate on it, a farce called *The Evil Eye,* and Scott wanted it to be as good as *Fie! Fie! Fi-Fi!*

But although he might have thought he'd be spending his time in St. Paul writing, a pleasant surprise awaited him. An old friend, Marie Hersey, had brought her roommate from college home with her, a girl named Ginevra King who lived in a wealthy Chicago suburb. At sixteen, she was beautiful, wealthy, and confident.

While at another time he might have felt outclassed, Scott was in top form that Christmas. He enjoyed the reputation among his St. Paul friends as a "fast Ivy League man" and was a celebrity because of the success of his play. He knew he wasn't perfect, but he felt he was a good match for Ginevra. "I didn't have the two

top things—great animal magnetism or money," he wrote in his journal. "I had the second things, though, good looks and intelligence. So I always got the top girl."[53]

Poor Boys Shouldn't Think of Marrying Rich Girls

True to his word, Scott interested Ginevra. The two met at a dance, flirted, then saw each other the following day before he had to return to Princeton. He was not worried that she had a string of older boyfriends already; on the contrary, he enjoyed the competition. Young women usually found him attractive, too, for he seemed to radiate a genuine interest in the things they talked about.

No matter how Ginevra felt about Scott that day as he caught the train back to Princeton, it is certain that he was totally in love with her—in a way he'd never been before. Scott knew how attractive she was and how other men pursued her. He wrote her worried letters each day—some of them twenty pages or more and so thick they had to be sent in a series of envelopes. Thus began a two-year romance—most of it conducted through the mail, although they saw each other on school holidays. Ginevra also came to Princeton in the spring of 1915 for the school prom (with her mother in tow as a chaperone).

He had, as it turned out, a great justification for his worry. In the spring of 1916 she was expelled from her college for talking to boys at night from her bedroom window. Scott tried not to let this change his feelings about her, but a rift in their relationship began soon afterward. He knew he was no longer the first in line for her affection, and

A Mentor

As Andre Le Vot notes in his book F. Scott Fitzgerald: A Biography, *the author greatly looked up to Edmund Wilson and thought of him as a mentor. Le Vot discusses their relationship through the years.*

"Fitzgerald . . . admired in Wilson the qualities he lacked in himself: his imperturbably objective judgment, his faculty for abstract reasoning, his easy honesty in handling concepts, and a seemingly exhaustive knowledge of literature that was constantly nourished by well-planned reading. The two young men immediately established a master-disciple relationship: humility and submission from Fitzgerald and, from Wilson, haughty irony and biting comments. But there was a balm for the wounds: the admission that this barbarian had talent, that although he committed every imaginable literary sin, there was an unquestionable vital energy in what he wrote. . . . Even when he was twenty years out of Princeton, Fitzgerald could still write to him after a brief reunion: 'Believe me, Bunny, it meant more to me than it could possibly have meant to you to see you that evening. It seemed to renew old times learning about Franz Kafka and latter things that are going on in the world of poetry, because I am still the ignoramus that you and John Bishop wrote about at Princeton.'"

Edmund Wilson (pictured) became one of Scott Fitzgerald's closest friends despite differences in their personalities and backgrounds.

it was remarked in his presence (it is not known by whom) that poor boys should not even think of marrying wealthy girls.

"She Was the First Girl I Ever Loved"

Not long afterward, Ginevra sent Scott an announcement that she was marrying a navy officer. The finality, as well as the impersonality of the announcement, broke his heart. It was a rejection that was to hurt him all his life.

As with other pain in his life, he used her in his writing, modeling many of the glamorous women of his novels and short stories after her—among them, Daisy in *The Great Gatsby* and Nicole in *Tender Is the Night*. But this didn't diminish his feelings of sadness and failure. Near the end of his life, Scott had an occasion to see Ginevra socially, and he wrote about it to his daughter: "She was the first girl I ever loved and I have faithfully avoided seeing her up to this moment to keep that illusion perfect, because she ended up by throwing me over with the most supreme boredom and indifference."[54]

Ginevra, as it turned out, divorced her first husband and married a second time, the heir of the Carson, Pirie, Scott department store fortune. She later denied feel-

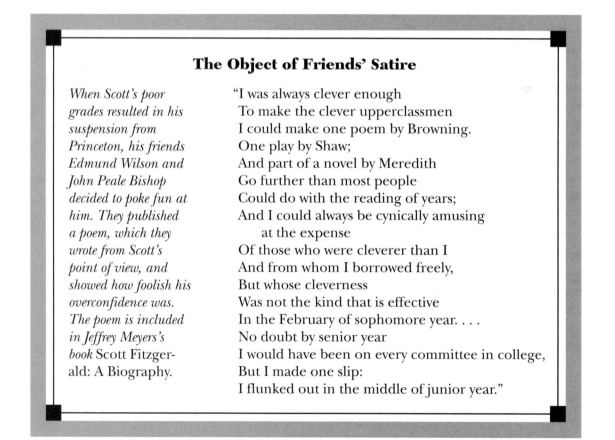

The Object of Friends' Satire

When Scott's poor grades resulted in his suspension from Princeton, his friends Edmund Wilson and John Peale Bishop decided to poke fun at him. They published a poem, which they wrote from Scott's point of view, and showed how foolish his overconfidence was. The poem is included in Jeffrey Meyers's book Scott Fitzgerald: A Biography.

"I was always clever enough
To make the clever upperclassmen
I could make one poem by Browning.
One play by Shaw;
And part of a novel by Meredith
Go further than most people
Could do with the reading of years;
And I could always be cynically amusing
     at the expense
Of those who were cleverer than I
And from whom I borrowed freely,
But whose cleverness
Was not the kind that is effective
In the February of sophomore year. . . .
No doubt by senior year
I would have been on every committee in college,
But I made one slip:
I flunked out in the middle of junior year."

ing anything special toward Scott, admitting that she was interested in attracting lots of boyfriends rather than being tied down to one:

> I can't remember even kissing Scott. I imagine I did. But it wasn't exactly a big thing in my life! . . . I guess I was too busy adding to my string to analyze my reaction to one suitor. . . . He was mighty young when we knew each other. I just never singled him out as anything special. . . . I was [later] engaged to two other people. That was very easy during the war because you'd never get caught. It was just covering yourself in case of a loss.[55]

Elections and Eating Clubs

But back at Princeton at the end of his sophomore year and still involved with Ginevra, Scott was a happy young man. It seemed that most of the things in his life were going as he had planned. The script he and Edmund Wilson had written for *The Evil Eye* was wonderful, and the Triangle Club elected him secretary for the following year. This especially pleased him, for holding the office of secretary as a junior would almost guarantee his being chosen president the next year.

He also achieved another social victory, an invitation to one of the prestigious "eating clubs" at Princeton. There were no fraternities at the college, but the eating clubs were similar in design; eighteen of them held nightly dinners and weekend parties in houses near the campus. As with fraternities, membership in the eating clubs was determined by popularity and social rank. Each of the clubs offered bids to

As a junior, Fitzgerald began to gain friends. Popularity was far more important to Fitzgerald than academic achievement.

about twenty-five men; one-quarter of the students did not receive invitations and continued to eat in the college dining room, suffering the humility of rejection.

Scott had been considered by the four most prestigious clubs: the Cottage, the Cap and Gown, Ivy, and Tiger Inn. In the end, it was the Cottage Club, whose president was Walker Ellis, that invited him to be a member. As he headed toward his junior year, things looked promising.

A Disaster

Scott's junior year started miserably. As the year before, he arrived on campus early in the fall to take makeup exams in three of the courses he had failed in his sophomore year. He failed two of the three exams, once again making it impossible for him to tour the following Christmas with *The Evil Eye*. However, this year's failure was even more disastrous: He was ineligible for all campus offices, including that of secretary (and later president) of the Triangle Club.

He was devastated. Hoping to change the mind of the faculty committee, a group of Triangle Club members petitioned the

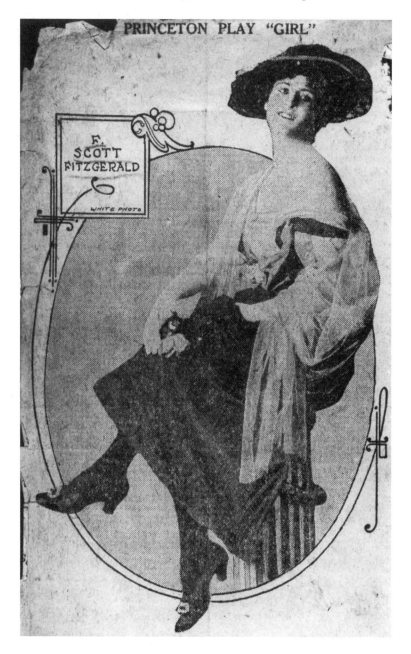

PRINCETON PLAY "GIRL"

F. SCOTT FITZGERALD

WHITE PHOTO

Fitzgerald dressed as a woman for his role in The Evil Eye. *Because of his poor grades, Fitzgerald was not allowed to tour with the play.*

"A Stunning Blonde in a Turquoise Gown"

When Scott's illness—combined with his poor grades—made him ineligible to participate in the Triangle Club tour in 1915–1916, he went home and spent time back in St. Paul. Bored one evening, he decided to don the chorus girl outfit he'd worn in the promotional posters for the show. The results were interesting, as Dave Page and John Koblas explain in F. Scott Fitzgerald in Minnesota: Toward the Summit.

"As a spoof, he masqueraded as a young lady, complete with dress and makeup, and attended a Psi Upsilon dance at the University of Minnesota on February 26. [A friend's sister] provided Fitzgerald with the feminine apparel, and Gus [the friend] acted as escort to the fraternity house, located at 1721 University Avenue S.E.

If he couldn't be the most beautiful showgirl in the Triangle Club, at least he could act the part in another venue. As a 'stunning blonde in a turquoise gown,' Fitzgerald spent the evening casually asking for cigarettes in the middle of the dance floor and absent-mindedly drawing a small vanity case from the top of a blue stocking. Freshmen were forced to take walks outside to cool themselves, while Fitzgerald filled his dance card with the names of 'all the popular fraternity men and best dancers.'

One version of the escapade has Fitzgerald escaping undetected after beguiling several male party goers into requesting a later rendezvous. Another suggests that Scott was caught when he tried to enter the men's restroom. In any event, the escapade made the front page of the following Monday's *St. Paul Daily News*. 'Mr. Fitzgerald, who is a Princeton student, at home on leave of absence,' the article said, 'has made a name for himself in college circles as an extremely successful female impersonator.'"

dean to allow Scott to at least tour with the club. After all, they reasoned, it was Scott's picture (as a sexy showgirl) they were running in newspapers all over the country as publicity for *The Evil Eye*. How could they not produce him in person to theatergoers? The faculty committee, however, remained unmoved. Scott could attend classes, he could write, he could even attend rehearsals, but he could not tour—and he could not hold office within the club.

Scott knew it was his own fault, but he remained bitter even twenty-five years later. "To me college would never be the same," he wrote. "There were to be no badges of pride, no medals, after all. It seemed . . . that I had lost every single thing I wanted."[56]

In November he caught malaria—not at all uncommon then because of the mosquitoes in the swamps around Princeton. He went to classes as long as he was able but left at the end of the month to recuperate. This spared him having to take his midyear exams—he was doing poorly in most of his classes again. Scott was extremely sensitive about failing at Princeton; the illness allowed him to save face. So raw a subject was it, in fact, that when his friend John Peale Bishop mentioned in 1937 that Scott had in fact failed out of Princeton, Scott became furious and even claimed that he had been carried out of his living quarters on a stretcher.

All of this, in addition to the end of his relationship with Ginevra, makes his journal entry for the year very understandable: "A year of terrible disappointments and the end of all college dreams," he wrote. "Everything bad was my own fault."[57]

The college authorities allowed him to return the following year—provided he repeat his junior year. His heart was not in it, however. He was failing three of his six classes by January 1917, but he wasn't paying much attention to his affairs at Princeton. He was only marking time.

4 War and Zelda

By the time the United States entered World War I in the spring of 1917, the Princeton campus was buzzing with interest in the war. Scott thought of enlisting, and in May he signed up for three weeks of training on campus.

It wasn't, as he readily admitted, that the conflict overseas concerned him one way or the other—it didn't. As he later wrote of the hero in *This Side of Paradise,* "Beyond a sporting of the German dash for Paris, the whole affair failed either to thrill or interest him. . . . He hoped it would be long and bloody." When the action stalled as the armies became mired in the trenches across France, he wrote, he felt "like an irate ticket holder at a prizefight where the principals refuse to mix it up."[58]

Yet many of his friends were enlisting. Edmund Wilson had signed on with a hospital unit and was being sent to France. John Peale Bishop had enlisted in the infantry and was awaiting his commission as a first lieutenant. In addition, the growing fervor on the campus made enlisting seem almost as heroic to Scott as the football team seemed.

"Please Let's Not Have Either Tragedy or Heroics"

Scott took exams to be an officer, and on October 26, 1917, his commission came through. Just as his first thought when finally admitted to Princeton was having his parents send his football gear from home, he now sent off a rush order to Brooks Brothers in New York so he could have finely tailored uniforms.

He also sent a letter to his mother warning her not to become teary and emotional about his going off to war; he told her that he was not going out of any patriotic fervor:

I'm too Irish for that—I may get killed for America—but I'm going to die for myself. . . . About the army, please let's not have either tragedy or Heroics because they are equally distasteful to me. I went into this perfectly cold-bloodedly and don't sympathize with the "Give my son to country". . . stuff because I *just went* and purely for *social reasons.*[59]

He was sent to Fort Leavenworth, Kansas, just northeast of Kansas City, for three months of basic training. Scott found within a few days that it was not as interesting as he had perhaps hoped. And just as he had done at Newman Academy and at Princeton when he was bored, he wrote during his classes. When his instructors discovered him writing during an infantry class, however, he was ordered not to write when he was supposed to be listening.

"I Had Only Three Months to Live"

The motivation for his writing at this time was a sense of impending disaster, which was common among young American men who were preparing to leave for war. "I had only three months to live," he wrote later. "In those days all infantry officers thought they had only three months to live—and I had left no mark on the world."[60]

His mark, he decided, was to be a novel, largely autobiographical, which he called *The Romantic Egotist*. (The title was suggested by his friend, Father Fay, with whom he'd stayed in contact since his days at the Newman Academy.) After he was caught writing in class, he spent every moment of his weekends scribbling in a corner of the Officers' Club at Fort Leavenworth.

As soon as he finished a chapter, he was eager for feedback; he sent off bits and pieces to several of his closest friends, including John Peale Bishop. Bishop was critical, saying that the novel seemed cluttered and lacked structure. He urged Scott to be more selective about which experiences he included in his writing.

Father Fay, Scott's mentor since his Newman days, was in Europe, but their mutual friend Shane Leslie was interested in the chapters Scott sent him. Leslie was far more supportive of the writing than Bishop was and encouraged Scott to put all of his youthful energy into the novel.

Heeding Leslie's advice, Scott devoted all his time to writing and revising his manuscript. When it was finished, he gave it to Leslie, who helpfully corrected grammatical and spelling mistakes before handing it to his own publisher, Charles Scribner.

Leslie attached a note highly recommending Scott as a young spokesman for his generation. He also noted that, while the manuscript had value already, "of course when he is killed it will also have a commercial value."[61]

A Poor Soldier

Meanwhile, the army was keeping Scott busy. After completing his basic training, he was ordered to report to the 45th Infantry Regiment in Louisville, Kentucky. After a short time there, he and his unit were sent to Camp Gordon in Georgia and then to Camp Sheridan, in Montgomery, Alabama, to prepare for overseas duty.

It was soon clear, however, that he was as poor a soldier as he had been a student. He was not well liked, for he seemed to his peers to be immature and irresponsible. They felt he lacked common sense and sound judgment—two necessities in a leader. As a result, few took him seriously, often pulling practical jokes and pranks on him.

One such prank was telling Scott that it would be wise for him to ignore reveille and sleep late, thereby being more awake for duty later in the day. When Scott realized his mistake and hurried to the commanding general's inspection, he was so nervous that he fell off his horse. In another incident, he took fellow officers' advice and forced a conscientious objector to pick up a rifle and participate in drills—an order that could have resulted in his own court-martial.

However, Scott did not seem to need others to lead him into trouble. While he was stationed in Georgia, he was given command of a mortar company and mis-

Caught up in the patriotism that surrounded the U.S. entry into World War I, Scott quickly enlisted and began training as a soldier in 1917.

by folding a dollar bill several times to make it look like a hundred, but to no avail.

Two Disappointments

In August 1917 Scribner's contacted Scott with bad news. They had rejected *The Romantic Egotist,* feeling that it lacked direction. One of the editors, Maxwell Perkins, thought that the manuscript had a great deal of promise, but his opinion was outweighed by that of the senior editors.

In a long letter—which was definitely not a form rejection letter—the editors explained that the story seemed to have no conclusion. They suggested that if Scott were to revise it, they would certainly consider it a second time. Unfortunately, Scott's revisions did not make the manuscript any more desirable to Scribner's; Maxwell Perkins sent a letter rejecting it, too, in October.

A second disappointment occurred a month later. Scott's regiment was ready to leave for France when the war ended on November 11, 1918. He had been spared making the ultimate sacrifice that twenty-one Princeton young men had made—5 percent of his class. But rather than being relieved that he wouldn't be part of the combat overseas, he was heartbroken.

He had hoped to have a heroic opportunity he had missed on the football fields of Princeton. Scott wrote later that his two biggest regrets of his youth were not being good enough to play football in college and not getting overseas during the war. He admitted feeling cheated; he met a friend in a bar after the armistice and complained: "God damn it to hell! I needed so much to get over. . . . I wanted to belong to

takenly directed the unit to fire on another unit on the firing range. And when ordered to supervise the unloading of supplies from a train in Hoboken, New Jersey, he left for a while to visit Princeton. Thousands of dollars' worth of equipment was stolen.

Scott even faced military arrest when he went to New York City for a party one evening. He borrowed a friend's room at the Hotel Astor and was caught by the management—naked and in bed with a girl. He tried to bribe the house detective

"Dog! Dog! Dog!"

One of the things Fitz- gerald's friends most liked about him was his quick wit and sense of humor. In the early 1920s, before alcoholism was a problem, he used to make up funny songs and sing them at parties. One of the most popular, called "Dog! Dog! Dog!" was written with the help of Edmund Wilson and is included in Matthew Bruccoli's Some Sort of Epic Grandeur: The Life of F. Scott Fitzgerald.

"In Sunny Africa they have the elephant
And in India they have the ze-ber-a—
Up in Canada the Rocky Mountain Goat
And in Idaho the shoat
(You've heard about it!)
But of all these animals
You will find the best of pals—
Is!

Dog, dog—I like a good dog—
Towser or Bowser or Star—
Clean sort of pleasure—
A four-footed treasure—
And faithful as few humans are!
Here, Pup: put your paw up—
Roll over dead like a log!
Larger than a rat!
More faithful than a cat!
Dog! Dog! Dog!"

what every other bastard belonged to: the greatest club in history. . . . They kept me out of it."[62]

Zelda

One aspect of military life that he did *not* regret was the social life. Scott had dated many girls since he had enlisted, enjoying the status an officer's uniform could bring.

As soon as he learned he was to be transferred to Camp Sheridan during the summer of 1918, Scott wrote to Lawton Campbell, an Alabaman whom he had known at Princeton, and asked for the name of the "fastest" girl in Montgomery. Campbell complied, mailing three names to Scott. However, it was not one of the names on Campbell's list who caught Scott's eye that summer; it was seventeen-year-old Zelda Sayre, a pretty blond who had just graduated from the local high school.

They met one evening in early July at a country club dance in Montgomery. He looked every bit the dashing officer, and she showed off her dancing ability in a performance of her favorite number, "Dance of the Hours." Scott asked to be introduced, and it was soon apparent that they were attracted to each other. Several Fitzgerald biographers have written that his sudden infatuation with Zelda was more of a case of love on the rebound, because he had just received, a month earlier, a wedding announcement from Ginevra King.

Whatever the case, it was not long before his journal was filled with entries such as "Fell in love with Zelda," "Stolen kisses on the stair," and "Discovery that Zelda's class voted her prettiest and most attractive."[63]

An Alabama Gypsy

Scott thought Zelda was the most beautiful girl he'd ever seen. Her hair was honey colored, and she had a perfect peaches-and-cream complexion. She had a straight nose and thin lips. Because of her erect posture, she seemed taller than five feet five inches. Scott used her as the model for Rosalind in his novel *This Side of Paradise* and described her this way:

> There was the eternally kissable mouth, small, slightly sensual and utterly disturbing. There were gray eyes and an unimpeachable skin with two spots of vanishing color. She was slender and athletic, without underdevelopment, and it was a delight to watch her move about a room.[64]

Zelda was the youngest of the five Sayre children; her three sisters were much older, and she had a brother who was six years older than she. Her father, Anthony

Scott met and fell in love with Zelda Sayre while he was stationed in Montgomery, Alabama, in 1918. Zelda's beauty and popularity captivated Scott.

A Legend in Montgomery

Zelda had a profound effect on men, especially as a teenager in her hometown of Montgomery, Alabama. In this excerpt from Scott Fitzgerald, *biographer Jeffrey Meyers explains the extent of her legendary power over the opposite sex.*

"Zelda's volatile mixture of beauty and daring was fatally attractive to men. Officers gathered on her sagging veranda, which resembled an army recruiting station, and gladly surrendered their military insignias to express their esteem. Flyers from Camp Sheridan performed aerial stunts over her house and two planes crashed during these daring exhibitions. Admirers at Auburn University, where she was tremendously popular, founded a fraternity based on her initials, Zeta Sigma. To be admitted, potential members had to pledge their devotion to Zelda and offer proof that they had had at least one date with her in Montgomery."

Flirtatious and beautiful, Zelda was sought after by many young men.

D. Sayre, was a justice of the Alabama Supreme Court for more than twenty years. Her mother, Minnie, was the daughter of a Kentucky senator and had once hoped to become an opera singer. Her father vetoed the idea; however, Minnie is said to have retained her imaginative, romantic spirit—evident in the naming of her youngest daughter. Zelda was a gypsy queen in Minnie's favorite book, *Zelda's Fortune*, written in 1874 by Robert Edward Francillon.

As the baby of the family, Zelda was pampered and spoiled, especially by her mother. "The Judge," as Zelda usually called her father, was a cold, austere man who preferred reading Homer, Juvenal, and other classical writers to talking with his children. He was a stickler for punctuality and lived his life by the clock. He always took the streetcar to and from work at exactly the same time each day and always went to bed as the hall clock chimed eight o'clock.

Making a Game of Disobeying Orders

But Zelda was nothing like her father. Although she loved him, she made a game out of disobeying his orders. In fact, in Montgomery she was known for being wild and unconventional. She smoked in public—a scandalous thing for a young woman to do—and drank as much and as often as boys her age did.

Her daredevil nature surfaced early in life. She later observed, "When I was a little girl I had great confidence in myself, even to the extent of walking by myself against life as it was then. I did not have a single feeling of inferiority, or shyness, or doubt, and no moral principles." [65]

The evidence seems to bear this out. When Zelda was ten, she phoned the fire department to report that there was a child trapped on the roof of her house. She then climbed up on the roof to await the rescuers—and the attention from her neighborhood. She also once climbed up into the driver's side of a carriage owned by one of her father's associates and took it for a fast ride down the street and back.

"Miserable and Ecstatic"

A great many young men desired Zelda, and this both excited and enraged Scott. He had always loved the idea of competition, and having the attention of a beautiful woman who was admired by others made her even more valuable in his eyes. Scott was especially proud that one of his chief rivals for Zelda's attention was an Auburn football star named Francis Stubbs—the kind of player he had admired at Princeton.

Scott pursued Zelda the entire summer of 1918, spending every moment he could get away from Camp Sheridan with her. He eventually worked himself up to number one on her list of boyfriends, and he wrote in his journal, "The most important year of life. Every emotion and any life work decided. Miserable and ecstatic, but a great success." [66]

Scott told her repeatedly how much he loved her, and Zelda said she loved him, too. They spent evenings on the front porch of her parents' house talking of the future—of the novels he would publish and how they would be married. But even though they shared such dreams, Zelda continued to date other men, a fact that drove Scott wild with jealousy.

The effect her flirtatiousness had on Scott was not lost on Zelda; in fact, she went to great lengths to let him know of her adventures. At a country club dance she once dragged a boy into a lighted phone booth and began kissing him. When the astonished boy asked her what she was doing, she told him that she knew Scott was coming and that she wanted to make him jealous. In a letter to Scott, Zelda confessed that she found him more appealing after he'd been angry with her: "I love your tenderness when I've hurt you. That's one of the reasons I could never be sorry for our quarrels."[67]

A Frustrating Courtship

October was a discouraging month for Scott. He learned that his revised version of *The Romantic Egotist* had been rejected by Scribner's. In addition, his regiment just missed being sent overseas; the signing of the armistice ended his hope of being part of the war.

When he and the other men of his unit were sent back to Montgomery for demobilization, Scott had mixed emotions. He was looking forward to spending more time with Zelda, but he felt like a failure. When he and Zelda began quarreling almost from the moment he arrived in Montgomery, he wondered whether the two of them had a future.

He was certain that he did not want to marry her. In a December 1918 letter to a friend, he wrote, "My affair still drifts. But my mind is firmly made up that I will not, shall not, can not, should not, must not marry—still, she *is* remarkable."[68]

But not long after that, he was certain that he *did* want marriage. He proposed, asking Zelda to marry him as soon as possible. She declined, however, claiming she was too young to be anyone's wife. Scott understood her sentiments and later used them in his descriptions of Rosalind in *This Side of Paradise*. Rosalind says, "I'm just a little girl. I like sunshine and pretty things and cheerfulness—and I dread responsibility. I don't want to think about pots and kitchens and brooms. I want to worry about whether my legs will get slick and brown when I swim in the river."[69]

Her other worry, she said, was that Scott would not make enough money to support a wife. After all, his novel had been turned down, and he seemed to have no prospects. Didn't it seem foolish to start off the marriage with no money to speak of? "Zelda was cagey about throwing in her lot with me before I was a money-maker,"[70] he later wrote.

"In the Land of Ambition and Success"

Discharged from the army and determined to win Zelda, Scott threw himself into the difficult task of making money. He left Montgomery for New York, vowing to return to marry her. He sent Zelda a telegram immediately: "WHILE I FEEL SURE OF YOUR LOVE, EVERYTHING IS POSSIBLE. I AM IN THE LAND OF AMBITION AND SUCCESS AND MY ONLY HOPE IS THAT MY DARLING HEART WILL BE WITH ME SOON."[71]

While Scott might have thought he could find work easily, he soon found out that jobs were hard to get. The prosperity of the last four years had been based on the war effort, and it collapsed within weeks after the government canceled most of its military contracts. Scott was one of 2 million soldiers who was searching for employment in the midst of a deepening recession. With the added handicap of his unremarkable record at Princeton, his chances of a well-paying job dwindled.

He decided to try the city rooms of the New York newspapers, hoping to find a job as a reporter. After being turned down by seven papers, he became discouraged. "All the confidence I had garnered at Princeton . . . melted gradually away," he wrote. "Lost and forgotten, I walked quickly away from certain places—from the pawn shop where one left the field glasses, from prosperous friends whom one met wearing the suit from before the war, from busy, cheerful offices that were saving the jobs for their own boys from the war—from restaurants after tipping with the last nickel."[72]

A History of Mental Illness

As an intimate friend of Scott Fitzgerald, Sheila Graham was well aware of the love he and Zelda had shared. In her book The Real F. Scott Fitzgerald: Thirty-Five Years Later, *she discusses the worrisome background of mental instability and madness in Zelda's family.*

"In hindsight it is easy to discern the germs of madness in Zelda's early behavior. I wonder that no one questioned it, especially given the mental instability in her mother's family. Minnie Machen's mother—Zelda's maternal grandmother—committed suicide when Zelda was a girl, but no one in the Sayre household ever mentioned this. Also Zelda's oldest sister Marjorie had suffered a nervous breakdown. And later on, after Zelda's own collapse, so did her brother Anthony. Finally afraid that he might kill his mother, he took his own life by jumping out a window. (In fact, [one biographer] has pointed out that there was mental illness on both sides of Zelda's family.)

Scott, however, had no doubts concerning Zelda's sanity before 1930—when he came home to their apartment in Paris to find her playing in a corner with some dirt. . . . I shivered when he described this scene. . . . It also seemed incredible to me that he should not have suspected earlier that she was obviously unstable. But the 20s were a crazy time . . . so that Zelda in its context was simply 'an original.' Those plunges into the Plaza Fountain—today she would have been carted off to Bellevue."

Living Poor

He finally settled for an unappealing job with the Barron Collier advertising agency at $90 a month. For four months he wrote slogans for streetcars; his best one, for a steam laundry in Iowa, was "We keep you clean in Muscatine." And although he had originally hoped to find a charming apartment in Greenwich Village, he settled for a dismal, poorly lit room near Columbia University in upper Manhattan.

Scott knew he would never get rich in advertising. His passion was still writing; on weekends and after work he labored over short stories, film scenarios, sketches, jokes, song lyrics—anything that might sell. But nothing sold, and he decorated the walls of his room with a mural made of 122 rejection slips.

The meager salary from the advertising agency did not go far, either. He learned very quickly what it was like to live on a shoestring budget. His social life in New York was almost nil. He ate his meals at the Yale-Princeton club and made a few friends there. However, he annoyed them more often than he amused them. Apparently seeking attention, he pulled pranks, such as taking a friend's hat and mixing hash, eggs, and ketchup in it.

As time went by and he became more discouraged about his lack of success in earning money as a writer, he frequently announced to some of the members of the Yale-Princeton club that he planned to commit suicide. They had become so bored listening to his complaints, however, they didn't take him seriously.

After countless rejections of his writing, Scott was able to sell a story, "Babes in the Woods," to a magazine called *Smart Set*.

He made $30 on the story, which was actually an old one from his Princeton days. Although he could have certainly applied the money to more basic needs, he bought a pair of white flannel pajamas for himself.

He also bought two presents for Zelda: a fan made of purplish feathers and some fancy pajamas. She was thrilled with the gifts, saying of the fan, "Those feathers—those wonderful, wonderful feathers are the most beautiful things on earth." The pajamas, she wrote, "are the most adorably moon-shiney things on earth—I feel like a *Vogue* cover in 'em."[73]

In March he sent her an engagement ring that had once belonged to his mother. Zelda sent him an excited letter immediately. "Scott Darling," she wrote, "It really is beautiful. . . . I've never worn a ring before, they've always seemed so inappropriate—but I love to see this shining there so nice and white like our love." And a few days later she reported that the ring had caused a stir at a party she'd attended the night before. "You can't imagine what havoc the ring wrought—A whole dance was completely upset last night."[74]

"I've Done My Best and I've Failed"

Scott continued to work for the advertising agency and write in his spare time. Although he and Zelda were officially engaged, it was painfully obvious by her letters that she was still dating—and enjoying every minute of it. He pressed her to set a wedding date, but she refused. She still was adamant about wanting him to have a successful career before she would consider marriage, although she denied that the

Even though she agreed to marry Fitzgerald, Zelda continued her flirtatious relationships with other suitors. Zelda became frustrated with Fitzgerald's possessiveness.

money mattered to her. "All the material things are nothing," she wrote. "I'd just hate to live a sordid, colorless existence—because you'd soon love me less—and less—and I'd do anything—anything to keep your heart for my own."[75]

As reassuring as this letter was, there were soon several letters, in which she wrote about dates with other men, that made him nervous and jealous. He continued his daily letters, complaining that he now understood why in fairy tales they used to lock princesses in towers. However, such talk made the situation worse, as Zelda's next letter indicated:

I'm so damned tired of being told that you "used to wonder why they kept princesses in towers"—you've written that, verbatim, in your last *six* letters! It's dreadfully hard to write so very much—and so many of your letters sound forced—I know you love me, Darling, and I love you more than anything in the world, but if it's going to be so much longer, we just *can't* keep up this frantic writing.[76]

Frantic now, Scott wrote to her explaining that he wanted to come for a visit. Being face to face, he thought, might help them resolve the problem. In her reply, however, Zelda infuriated Scott by telling him how busy she would be at that time and how difficult it would be to work his visit into her hectic schedule. She had been invited to senior prom at Georgia Tech and to the commencement exercises shortly afterward.

Zelda expected to be quite tired after that. "They always dance till breakfast," she confided to Scott. He made the trip anyway and tried to convince her once again to marry him. This time, however, she not only refused but broke the engagement. Distraught, Scott went back to New York and promptly wrote a letter to a friend. "I've done my best and I've failed," he confessed. "It's a great tragedy and I feel I have very little left to live for. . . . I wish you'd tear up this letter and I know you'll never say what I told you in an hour of depression. Unless someday she will marry me I will never marry."[77]

Chapter

5 Early Success

The immediate result of his breakup with Zelda was a monthlong drinking binge. He ended up visiting a friend in Boston, just in time for national Prohibition to take effect on the first day of July 1919.

He knew, as he sobered up, that New York was not the place he wanted to be. The drab, grimy room and the uninteresting job had no purpose without a love in his life, and he gave notice to his advertising agency at once. As he wrote in 1937, "I quit work or, if you prefer, I retired from business. I was through. . . . I retired not on my profits, but on my liabilities, which included debts, despair, and a broken engagement and crept home to St. Paul to 'finish a novel.'" [78]

To a casual observer, it might not have seemed so bad, licking his wounds in the comfort of his parents' lovely Summit Avenue home. But for Scott the return was an admission of defeat, and for a young man who had wanted more than anything to be viewed as successful, his circumstances were humiliating. He viewed this time as a last chance; he knew he had lost Zelda, and if he could not write successfully, he would have lost everything.

There were a few things that gave him some hope. On the train from New York to St. Paul he had read a current bestseller called *Fortitude* by Hugh Walpole. He thought it was terrible, and it made him confident that he could do infinitely better himself.

Scott's parents were pleased to see him but not supportive of his literary ambitions—especially his mother. She tried securing him a job as an advertising manager of a local wholesaler and was upset when her son turned down the offer. Even so, Edward and Mollie Fitzgerald allowed him to take over the front room on the third floor for his writing.

Cigarettes and Coke

Scott wrote with a fierce determination that summer, sometimes working fifteen or more hours each day. When he was hungry, he would not leave his room but would use the servants' bell hanging just around the corner to attract his mother's attention, ordering meals or other necessities by means of the speaking tube. To save space on his overcrowded writing desk, he neatly pinned his chapter outlines to the curtains. When he needed to have a few moments of rest, he could lift the window, unlatch the screen, and crawl out on the ledge.

That summer he swore off drinking, often a crutch when he was depressed. It

Fitzgerald worked furiously to complete his novel The Romantic Egotist *in the summer of 1919. Fitzgerald hoped to win Zelda back by becoming a published writer.*

wasn't because of Prohibition that he made the decision—St. Paul was, actually, one of the easiest places in the country to secure bootleg liquor, so he could have procured it if he had wanted to. His motivation was to finish the novel, and if he drank he would not concentrate. Instead he smoked and drank Coke and occasionally walked down to W. A. Frost's pharmacy with his childhood friend Tubby Washington, who often lent the always-broke Scott change for cigarettes or a chocolate bar.

Waiting

By the end of July, Scott was confident that his novel would soon be ready for Scribner's. He wrote Maxwell Perkins to tell him that he'd finished the first draft, which he explained included some of the material from his ill-fated *The Romantic Egotist*. However, Scott assured Perkins, the new novel was by no means another revision of the earlier work. Scott said that the title would be *The Education of a Personage*, but a few weeks later he wrote Perkins again to inform him that he had changed the title to *This Side of Paradise*. Perkins responded enthusiastically to the news that Fitzgerald was writing again and said that he was looking forward to seeing the manuscript. Scott wrote also to his old friend Edmund Wilson, telling him of his completed novel.

Although he was optimistic about his writing, Scott was gloomy about his chances of winning Zelda back. "I'll tell you what the situation is now," he wrote. "I wouldn't care if she died, but I couldn't stand to have anybody else marry her." [79]

After submitting the manuscript, Scott had nothing much to do except wait. Tired of being without spending money, he decided to get a job—any job. He talked to Larry Boardman, an old friend from his Elizabethan drama club days, and Boardman was able to pull strings at the Northern Pacific Railroad. Scott was hired on as a menial laborer, nailing the roofs on railroad

A First Try at Menial Labor

While waiting for his publishers to decide the fate of his novel This Side of Paradise, *Scott took a job with Northern Pacific Railroad in St. Paul. He worked on top of the cars, nailing roofing. Later, in a short story called "Forging Ahead," he wrote of his first confrontation with menial labor. A portion of that story, excerpted here, appears in* F. Scott Fitzgerald in Minnesota: Toward the Summit *by Dave Page and John Koblas.*

"At 6:30 the following morning, carrying his lunch, and a new suit of overalls that had cost four dollars, he strode self-consciously into the Great Northern car shops. It was like entering a new school, except that no one showed any interest in him or asked him if he was going out for the team. He punched a time clock, which affected him strangely, and without even an admonition from the foreman to 'go in and win,' was put to carrying boards for the top of the car.

Twelve o'clock arrived; nothing had happened. The sun was blazing hot and his hands and back were sore, but no real events had ruffled the dull surface of the morning. The president's little daughter had not come by, dragged by a runaway horse; not even a superintendent had walked through the yard and singled him out with an approving eye. Undismayed, he toiled on—you couldn't expect much the first morning."

cars. The work was unpleasant; his boss yelled at him the first day for sitting down rather than squatting while nailing. He was also chastised for not wearing blue jeans, which the other workers wore. The second day he got his new blue jeans stolen.

"We Are All for Taking a Chance"

If he knew how his manuscript was being received at Scribner's, Scott would surely have been very nervous. The editorial staff had been divided about the book; only Maxwell Perkins supported the manuscript. The other editors felt it was frivolous and uninteresting—Charles Scribner himself vowed that he could not put his name on any book that was without literary merit.

In the end, Perkins put his job on the line during an editorial meeting. "My feeling is that a publisher's first allegiance is to talent," he told them. "And if we aren't going to publish a talent like this, it is a very serious thing. . . . If we're going to turn down the likes of Fitzgerald, I will lose all interest in publishing books."[80]

Scribner reconsidered; Perkins got his way and sent off a letter informing Scott that Scribner's had decided to publish *This Side of Paradise*:

I am very glad, personally, to be able to write you that we are all for publishing your book, "This Side of Paradise." Viewing it as the same book that was here before, which in a sense it is, though translated into somewhat different terms and extended further, I think that you have improved it enormously. . . . The book is so different that it is hard to prophesy how it will sell but we are all for taking a chance and supporting it with vigor.[81]

Euphoria

Scott was almost delirious with happiness when he received the letter. Years later in a short story called "Early Success," he recalled his emotions that day in September:

Then the postman rang, and that day I quit work and ran along the streets, stopping automobiles to tell friends and acquaintances about it. That week the postman rang and rang, and I paid off my terrible small debts, bought a suit, and woke every morning with a world of ineffable toploftiness and promise.[82]

He would receive money for the book, of course; however, it would not be published until the following spring. He had quit his job at the Northern Pacific, for he had no interest in earning money doing anything except writing. His hope was that he could resume writing short stories on the strength of his novel's acceptance.

Scott returned to New York and began his new life as a "professional writer." Buoyed by confidence, he turned out new stories and revised old ones that had been so widely rejected just months before by changing titles, altering details, and resubmitting them. Some of these stories were accepted by the same editors who had previously rejected them. In just a few weeks he was making money, and his image of himself as a professional writer had been solidified.

Back to Zelda

He arranged for an agent to handle his business affairs and the selling of his short stories. This was a young man named Harold Ober, who remained Scott's agent throughout his life. Ober was a go-getter and soon sold two of Scott's reworked (and previously rejected) stories for $1,400. It was not only *Smart Set* that published his stories but also the prestigious and well-paying *Saturday Evening Post, Collier's,* and *Cosmopolitan.*

Each time he sold a story, he sent a telegram to Zelda—he knew that he had become successful enough for her. When he finally got the nerve to talk to her in person, he wired her a message that he was coming for a visit in November. Zelda responded enthusiastically. "I'm mighty glad you're coming," she wrote. "I've been waiting to see you (which you probably knew) but I *couldn't* ask you. . . . It's fine and I'm tickled to death." [83]

Their reunion was pleasant, although they did not officially resume their engagement. Even so, Scott was hopeful that he

Fitzgerald reported each early publishing success to Zelda in hopes of regaining her affection. Zelda, in turn, kept up a mild flirtation with Fitzgerald.

could win Zelda again. When he returned to New York, he wrote what some critics think of as one of his best short stories, "The Ice Palace," which drew upon his experiences with Zelda that November. It is the story of a beautiful southern belle who wants to leave home and journeys to Minnesota to visit her fiancé.

Zelda wrote to him not long after he returned to New York, and their intimate correspondence resumed. This time Scott was careful to contain any annoyance he felt at her flirtatious ramblings. She hadn't changed in that regard; she informed him cheerfully that she had recently been dating Auburn's starting quarterback. She also admitted that she hadn't really believed Scott could be successful as a writer but she had certainly changed her mind. "I am very proud of you—I hate to say this, but I don't *think* I had much confidence in you at first. . . . It's so nice to know that you really *can* do things." [84]

During that same month Scott began earning even more money. He sold four of his short stories to the *Saturday Evening Post* at fees of $500 apiece. Late in February, he sold the movie rights to one of the stories, "Head and Shoulders," to Metro Studios for the staggering price of $2,500. He promptly bought Zelda an expensive platinum and diamond watch he had seen

---

Unwelcome Fashion Advice

When Zelda first came to New York to be with Scott before their wedding, he noticed that her wardrobe was unsuitable for the glamorous metropolitan life he was planning on. In this excerpt from F. Scott Fitzgerald: A Biography, Andre Le Vot describes how that situation was remedied—as well as Zelda's reactions to it.

"In 1920 the chrysalis became a butterfly. Zelda was out of her usual element—where . . . women still maintained prewar traditions and fashions—and, despite her quickness, her frills and flounces jarred a bit on New York elegance. Scott contacted Marie Hersey, his old friend from St. Paul, who had gone to Vassar and knew New York well. He asked her to steer Zelda through the chic shops and tactfully persuade her to change her wardrobe. The first thing bought was a Patou suit, which, feeling strange, she charged to Scott for the first time. Thirteen years later she came across the suit, badly moth-eaten, in a trunk; [Zelda] noted that 'we are glad—oh, so relieved, to find it devastated at last.'

Her apprenticeship was brief; she did not have to put up for long with another woman's advice. Soon she had shed her provincial excesses and set out to conquer New York with nothing but her velvety Southern accent, the dissonances in her line of chatter and a coarse, roughneck bluntness."

---

in one of the luxurious Fifth Avenue shop windows; nothing mattered as much as convincing her he was truly able to support a wife. She was delighted and wrote, "O, Scott, it's so be-au-ti-ful—and the back's just as pretty as the front. . . . I've turned it over four hundred times to see 'from Scott to Zelda.'" [85]

"It Will Take More than the Pope to Make Zelda Good"

In March Zelda was going to visit Scott; the two were to meet at Princeton's Cottage Club (he wanted to be at Princeton when *This Side of Paradise* finally came out). Although she had indicated more strongly that she planned to marry him, Zelda still was hesitant to set a date. On the day she was to arrive, he received the first copy off the press of *This Side of Paradise,* and he told a friend who inquired about her that he felt they would soon announce a date.

He was right. She agreed that the time had come to marry; they set a date of April 3 for the wedding. Although he was ecstatic that she was finally going to go through with it, his happiness was marred somewhat by his feeling that some of his friends disapproved of her. One such friend was Isabelle Amorous, an old friend since his days at Newman Academy. Scott tried to convince Isabelle of Zelda's good qualities in a letter:

> Any girl who gets stewed in public, who frankly enjoys and tells shocking stories, who smokes constantly and makes the remark that she has "kissed thousands of men and intends to kiss thousands more," cannot be considered beyond reproach even if above

it. But Isabelle, I fell in love with her courage, her sincerity, and her flaming self-respect. [86]

The wedding took place in the vestry of St. Patrick's Cathedral in New York. Zelda wore a suit of midnight blue with a hat to match—she had no interest in a traditional wedding gown and veil. Although Zelda's parents had worried about Scott's suitability as a husband, they gave their blessing. They were not worried, as some of their friends were, about Scott's Catholic background. "A good Catholic is as good as any other man, and that is good enough," wrote Minnie Sayre to Scott. But she warned him that her daughter would be a difficult woman to be married to. "It will take more than the Pope to make Zelda good," she said; "you will have to call on God Almighty direct!" [87]

Kudos from Critics

That spring Scott must have felt as though he had achieved a great deal. Not only had he finally won the young woman he had set his heart on, but his first novel was just coming out.

He was naively optimistic about the sales of *This Side of Paradise,* believing that fame and fortune would soon be his. "I told the Scribner Company that I didn't expect my novel to sell more than twenty thousand copies," he recalled, "and when the laughter died away I was told that a sale of five thousand was excellent for a first novel." [88] Surprisingly, however, he was correct. Within the first week, twenty thousand copies of the book were sold, and that amount doubled the first year.

Scott finally convinced Zelda to marry him in 1920, after the publication of This Side of Paradise.

The reaction from the critics was largely enthusiastic. "If you have not already done so," wrote the book editor of the *Chicago Daily News,*

> make note of the name of F. Scott Fitzgerald. It is borne by a 23-year-old novelist who will, unless I am much mistaken, be much heard of hereafter.

His first novel, *This Side of Paradise* gives him, I think, a fair claim to membership in that small squad of contemporary American fictionists who are producing literature . . . it bears the impress, it seems to me, of genius.[89]

The best for F. Scott Fitzgerald, it appeared early in 1920, was just beginning.

Chapter

6 Fame and Fortune

Many critics point out that *This Side of Paradise* was an expression of what post–World War America was about. The country was bored by politics and public affairs. What appealed was fun, spontaneity, and good times—which Fitzgerald called "the Jazz Age." In the novel, he gave a realistic glimpse into new, liberated young women of the time—called "flappers"—who wore their hair scandalously short, smoked in public, and dared to show their knees. And because the book was largely autobiographical, it was not difficult to see that Zelda was the inspiration behind such women.

Living the Life

This Side of Paradise describes a glittering, gaudy world, and the young blond author and his beautiful wife looked as though they'd stepped right out of its pages. "He was handsome and casually graceful," observes one biographer; "he loved to be popular and blossomed with success. . . . He seemed, in his own person, a triumphant justification of the lifestyle his book recommended. So too did Zelda." [90]

Looking the part was not enough for the Fitzgeralds; they spent the first months of their marriage living the life so skillfully described in the book. The first priority for them was fun, and that usually entailed the lavish spending of money.

"Caution" did not seem to be in his vocabulary. At one party, Scott invited some of his Princeton friends to help him celebrate the publication of his novel:

> They found him in his room at the Knickerbocker Hotel, already a little drunk and surrounded by valets helping him get ready for the party; twenty- and fifty-dollar bills were crammed partway into his pockets with enough left showing to let everyone see that he was rich. [91]

They rented a suite at the Biltmore Hotel and entertained an almost nonstop stream of friends. More often than not, these impromptu get-togethers deteriorated into drinking parties, with the newest and most fashionable cocktail, the Orange Blossom (a mixture of orange juice and bootleg gin).

A Growing Problem

Although their lifestyle might have indicated otherwise, money was a difficulty for the Fitzgeralds. To pay the bills, Scott began

The Flapper

In F. Scott Fitzgerald: A Biography, *Andre Le Vot explains the radical change that women were experiencing in the 1920s. The "new woman" in society was known as the flapper, and with her boyish haircut and short skirts she was almost unrecognizable from the young women of a generation before.*

"[The changes in women brought about] the destruction of . . . the violin-shaped woman, full-breasted, wasp-waisted, lavishly hipped, a pizzicato creature, languorous and swooning, reclusive, idle, living only for the moment when marriage and maternity at last brought out her true self. Now she was being replaced by the clarinet woman: youthful, strident and boyish, a little piping, a little acid, unmysterious and disillusioned; she vied with and matched men at sports, at work, in love, expecting nothing from them but confirmation of her independence. In love duets it was she who chose the key and sounded the A. The new woman rejected boredom and monotony. She wanted to be entertained, and her partner had to turn wizard, change the humdrum into something magical, transform life itself."

Fitzgerald's novels defined the Jazz Age, including the infamous 1920s flappers—pictured here in a 1926 Charleston contest.

Although Scott's popularity as a writer earned him a steady income, he and Zelda's wild lifestyle still left them with little money.

sult of alcohol. However, there was a difference in the way the two handled liquor. Zelda drank because she enjoyed it. Scott was an alcoholic, dependent on drinking to function. In one of his later essays, he wrote, "About the time I came into some money I found that with a few drinks I got expansive and somehow had the ability to please people, and the idea turned my head. Then I began to take a whole lot of drinks to keep going and have everybody think I was wonderful." [92]

As time went on it became apparent that Zelda was especially unhappy. She had been part of a solid, staid family in Alabama who provided for her every need. Although headstrong and independent, she still had parents to whom she was accountable. Life with Scott was unpredictable—sometimes impossibly so.

Not a Housekeeper

As long as they were in hotels, they did not have to worry about cleaning and cooking. However, they were evicted from these hotels for the disruption they caused; in one hotel they annoyed guests by having contests in the hallways to see who could walk on their hands the farthest.

The Fitzgeralds then decided to move into a cottage in Westport, Connecticut, with the idea of saving money and providing a quiet place for Scott to work on his second novel. However, Zelda was forced to become a housekeeper, and she despised it. Mountains of dirty laundry piled up until neither of them had anything to wear. Scott, who prided himself on flashy dressing, was annoyed when he had no clean clothes, and they would fight. Visitors

borrowing money against future royalties or his "next novel" at Scribner's. This was a habit he would keep his whole life, say biographers.

They could easily have lived on the royalties from his novel if they had stayed on a budget. But the new clothes, the lavish automobiles, and the constant parties drained their finances. Scott continued to borrow against work he hadn't yet done, and this put the Fitzgeralds deeper in the hole.

Drinking was becoming more of a problem, too. Zelda drank along with Scott, and most of their social activities were the re-to their home commented on the disorganization and messiness of the place, noting unmade beds, filthy dishes from days before, and overflowing ashtrays.

The cottage was also intended as a quiet place for Scott to write. Unfortunately, however, the friends and wild times that had surrounded them in New York City followed them to Westport, turning their home, complained Scott, into a roadhouse.

"God Damn the Continent of Europe"

Early in February 1921 Zelda discovered she was pregnant, and for a month or two she lost a great deal of energy. When she started feeling better, she and Scott decided to plan a trip to Europe before she was too far into her pregnancy to travel comfortably. Scott rushed through the first draft of his manuscript, titled *The Beautiful and Damned,* so he could get another advance.

They sailed in early May, docking a week later in Southampton, England. The Scribner's London representative arranged for them to meet other authors and critics, and the London release of *This Side of Paradise* was to take place while they were there. However, they were disappointed in the reception it received. One London literary supplement remarked that "As a novel, it is rather tiresome." [93]

In addition to the humiliation he felt at the poor reviews, Scott was bored with endless sightseeing trips. He wrote to his friend Edmund Wilson, "God damn the continent of Europe. . . . France made me sick. Its silly pose as the thing the world has to save. I think it's a shame that England and America didn't let Germany conquer Europe." [94]

Not surprisingly, the Fitzgeralds cut their trip short and sailed home in relief.

From Montgomery to St. Paul

Zelda had hoped to wait out her pregnancy at home in Montgomery, being pampered by her family. However, Alabama was too hot for Zelda to endure. In addition, she was angry that southern manners required noticeably pregnant women to stay secluded indoors, away from public scrutiny. In typical Zelda fashion, she horrified neighbors by donning a large bathing suit and swimming in a local pool. Zelda was asked to leave, and she was furious.

After being there only a month, the Fitzgeralds went to St. Paul, where their baby daughter was born on October 26. As Scott wished, they named her after himself—Frances Scott Key Fitzgerald, or "Scottie" for short. Zelda, who had wanted to name the child Patricia, stubbornly called her "Pat" as a nickname until she was in first grade.

It didn't take Zelda long to tire of living in St. Paul. Caring for a baby was more work than Zelda was used to, and she was unhappy about experiencing winter in Minnesota. The subzero temperatures and drifting snow were distasteful to the young woman who had been raised in the warm Alabama sunshine.

The Beautiful and Damned

In March the Fitzgeralds left St. Paul and returned to New York. Their arrival was well timed, coinciding with the publication of *The Beautiful and Damned*. Like his first novel, this drew heavily on his experiences with Zelda, describing the unraveling of the marriage of Anthony and Gloria. They are pampered, beautiful people who move from that life to one of damnation—largely because of alcohol.

Sales of the book were fairly good; in the first year it sold more than forty thousand copies. Unfortunately, Scott had borrowed $5,600 against the book by the time it was published, so he was still in debt. He was forced to write more short stories. These paid the bills, although he

---

"We Hadn't a Notion What We Were"

During the first few months of their marriage, Zelda and Scott Fitzgerald were building a reputation in the gossip columns as a wild, zany couple who would do anything for their own amusement, no matter how irreverent. In this excerpt from Invented Lives: F. Scott and Zelda Fitzgerald, *author James Mellow describes how that reputation was achieved in New York City.*

"As devotees of the theater, the Fitzgeralds were a menace. They were quite likely to give more dramatic performances than what was going on behind the proscenium. (It was an old habit with Zelda, who, even when she was 'not one bit drunk or disorderly,' used to gossip so much with her friends in the Montgomery theaters that the performers stopped the orchestra.) At the performance of *George White's Scandals*, Fitzgerald upstaged the actors by doing the scandalous—undressing in public. He managed to get down to his undershirt before the ushers escorted him outside. At the comedy *Enter Madame*, the Fitzgeralds and their guests laughed at their own jokes instead of the playwright's. Zelda fell off her seat; the actors complained; the management asked them to leave. Zelda stormed out in a huff, trailed by Scott.

The Fitzgeralds made splashy appearances in the gossip columns: Zelda later took a plunge in a downtown public fountain. . . . Fitzgerald, not to be outdone, re-created the event in the chic uptown waters of the Pulitzer Fountain, outside the Plaza Hotel. They soon found themselves for a new generation of gilded youth. Later in his life, in a reminiscence titled 'My Lost City,' Fitzgerald stated, disingenuously, that the role had been thrust on them and that they found it confusing: 'Within a few months after our embarkation on the Metropolitan venture, we scarcely knew any more who we were and we hadn't a notion what we were.'"

The Fitzgeralds moved to New York in March 1922 after the birth of their daughter, Frances Scott Key Fitzgerald, in 1921.

always felt as though he were compromising himself to write for magazines.

He and Zelda had no one to blame for their money problems but themselves, however. In 1922 Scott made the exorbitant amount of $36,000—about twenty times what the average American worker made. They should have been able to live extremely well.

But they spent money extravagantly. For instance, Scott wrote to Maxwell Perkins at Scribner's asking for another loan of $1,500 against *The Beautiful and Damned* when he was being nagged by Zelda. "My family seems to need a fur coat," he explained. He used this episode in his book to show the growing lack of communication between Gloria and Anthony:

Throughout the previous winter one small matter had been a subtle and omnipresent irritant—the question of Gloria's gray fur coat. At that time women enveloped in long squirrel wraps could be seen every few yards along Fifth Avenue. The women were converted to the shape of tops. They seemed porcine and obscene; they resembled kept women in the concealing richness, the feminine animality of the garment. Yet—Gloria wanted a gray squirrel coat.[95]

Great Neck

In October 1922 Scott, Zelda, and Scottie moved to Great Neck, an affluent town on the north shore of Long Island, about an hour from downtown Manhattan. Their goal in moving to Great Neck was similar to that when they moved to Westport—to get away from the wild drinking parties so Scott could write. They hired a Swedish couple as cook and handyman, and a nurse to take care of the baby. They even bought a dog, which they named Fritzie.

Great Neck in the early 1920s was home to a number of important theater people, newspaper columnists, musicians, and writers. Such famous celebrities as George M. Cohan, Groucho Marx, Basil Rathbone, and Ring Lardner had homes near the Fitzgeralds'. Scott was positively dazzled, and the vows to stay sober evaporated as the parties occurred, one after another.

When the Fitzgeralds were not socializing with their new neighbors, they were

F. Scott Fitzgerald (far right) was known for the wild, excessive parties that he and Zelda gave at their home in Great Neck.

extending invitations to their friends in the city to come for the weekend. Soon the house was filled with guests, some staying well past the weekend. It was a common sight for drunken guests to pass out on the lawn of the Fitzgeralds' home and remain there until the next morning.

Although Scott was drinking more and therefore not doing much writing, he earned $10,000 in the sale of *This Side of Paradise* to a movie company. The writing he did do was a play that he called *The Vegetable*, the story of a railroad clerk whose wife wants him to be president, but he dreams of being a mailman.

Failure and Resolutions

Scott hoped the play would make him a fortune. He sent a copy to his friend Edmund Wilson, who thought it was the best American comedy ever written. Theatergoers, unfortunately, didn't share Wilson's assessment. When it opened on November 10, 1923, in Atlantic City, most of the audience walked out before the second act. Scott was terribly disappointed in the response.

The next week the play closed, and along with it the hope of the fortune he'd

"I Simply Can't and Won't"

In February 1920 Zelda suspected that she was pregnant. Distraught, she contacted Scott, who secured some pills that he was told would bring on menstruation. When Zelda received the pills, however, she had a change of heart, and wrote to Scott about it. This excerpt of that letter is included in The Correspondence of F. Scott Fitzgerald, *edited by Matthew Bruccoli and Margaret Duggan.*

"Dearest—

I wanted to for your sake, because I know what a mess I'm making and how inconvenient it's all going to be—but simply *can't* and *won't* take those awful pills—so I've thrown them away. I'd rather take carbolic acid. You see, as long as I feel that I had the right, I don't much mind what happens—and besides, I'd rather have a *whole family* than sacrifice my self-respect. They just seem to place everything on the wrong basis—and I'd feel like a damned whore if I took even one, so you'll try to understand, please Scott—and do what you think best—but don't do ANYTHING till we *know* because God—or something—has always made things right, and maybe this will be.

I love you, Darling Scott, and you love me, and we can be thankful for that anyway—

Zelda Sayre"

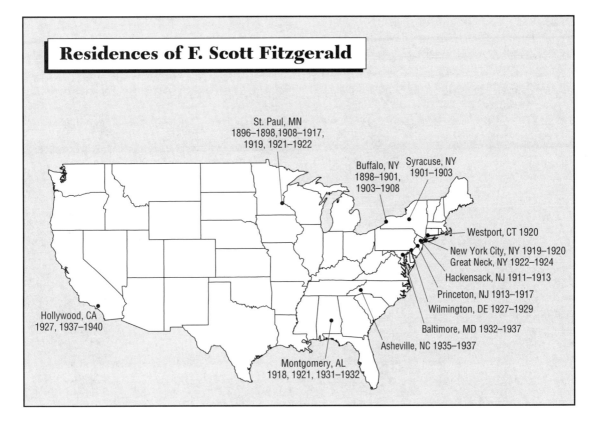

Residences of F. Scott Fitzgerald

St. Paul, MN
1896–1898,1908–1917,
1919, 1921–1922

Buffalo, NY
1898–1901,
1903–1908

Syracuse, NY
1901–1903

Westport, CT 1920

New York City, NY 1919–1920
Great Neck, NY 1922–1924

Hackensack, NJ 1911–1913

Princeton, NJ 1913–1917

Wilmington, DE 1927–1929

Baltimore, MD 1932–1937

Asheville, NC 1935–1937

Hollywood, CA
1927, 1937–1940

Montgomery, AL
1918, 1921, 1931–1932

planned to make from it. Doing what he always did when faced with financial crisis, he stopped drinking, isolated himself (this time in an empty room above the garage at Great Neck), and began writing short stories. He worked more or less steadily from late November until April, completing—and selling—eleven stories.

His effort earned him $17,000, and he promptly decided that a change was necessary. They could not go on with their extravagant lifestyle in Great Neck; they simply couldn't afford it. Scott also realized that the marathon writing sessions with the reliance on caffeine and cigarettes weren't good for him. He had a hacking cough and a bad case of insomnia, and he claimed that it took him more than six months to recover.

Europe, their friends were telling them, was far cheaper. Scott could begin a new novel and they could make a fresh start, away from the drinking and the foolishness of New York and Great Neck. "We were going to the Old World," recalled Fitzgerald later, "to find a new rhythm for our lives, with a true conviction that we had left our old selves behind forever." [96]

"Something Had Happened that Could Never Be Repaired"

The Fitzgeralds had not enjoyed their first trip to Europe, so they were anxious to find new spots to visit. They spent time in

Paris and ended up in St. Raphael on the Riviera, in a $79-a-month villa with a nanny for Scottie. Scott got to work on his next novel, *The Great Gatsby*. Things seemed to be moving along well, until July.

It was then that Zelda became involved with a handsome Frenchman—an aviator named Edouard Jozan. He was one of several young men whom the Fitzgeralds had met at the nearby cafes in the evening. Al-

The Fitzgeralds pose with their daughter Scottie during Christmas in Paris in 1925.

His Own Writing System

In Scott Fitzgerald, *biographer Jeffrey Meyers emphasizes that even though drinking was a problem for the author, he labored at his writing. In this excerpt, Meyers explains the method Fitzgerald used when working on a novel or story.*

"Despite his dissipation, Fitzgerald was a very hard worker. During his lifetime he published four novels (another remained unfinished and appeared posthumously), four volumes of short fiction, a play, and three hundred stories, articles and poems in magazines. He wrote in pencil with his left hand and had a large, loopy handwriting that looked like a child's. He often composed in the evenings, clouded by the smoke of Chesterfields and propelled (according to whether or not he was drinking) by astonishing quantities of gin or Coca-Cola. He made several drafts, depending on the importance of the work, before sending it out to a secretary to be typed. In 1922 his St. Paul friend Thomas Boyd reported that Fitzgerald's original drafts were (like his character) spontaneous and impulsive:

> 'Fitzgerald's writing is never thought out. He creates his characters and they are likely to lead him into almost any situation. His phrasing is done in the same way. It is rare that he searches for a word. Most of the time words come to his mind and they spill themselves in a riotous frenzy of song and color all over the page. Some days he writes as many as 7,000 or 8,000 words; and then, with a small *Roget's Thesaurus,* he carefully goes over his work, substituting synonyms for any unusual words that appear more than once in seven or eight consecutive pages.'"

though Zelda had always flirted (usually to make Scott jealous), this time it was different, for Scott knew nothing of what was going on.

Everyone knew about the affair . . . and could not mistake the relationship of Zelda and Edouard when they saw them on the beach together, or dancing at the casino. Only Scott, working with a joy he had rarely felt before, seemed unaware of what was going on. He was used to seeing Zelda flirt, but she usually did it so outrageously and so innocently that the very exuberance she brought to it absolved her of any guilty intent.[97]

Zelda came to Scott and asked for a divorce, which he refused to agree to. He later said that he demanded a confrontation with Jozan, but the Frenchman refused. The crisis passed—on the surface, at least—but the event left a permanent scar on their marriage. As Scott wrote in his ledger early that autumn, "I knew something had happened that could never be repaired."[98]

7 The Unraveling

Although upset by Zelda's infidelity, Scott continued his writing. He had vowed to himself to stay sober while working on *The Great Gatsby,* and he kept his promise. In November the manuscript was finished, and he sent it off to Maxwell Perkins in New York.

The novel, which borrows heavily from Scott's and Zelda's experiences with high living in Great Neck, drew immediate praise from Perkins. "I think you have every kind of right to be proud of this book," Perkins wrote. "It is an extraordinary book, suggestive of all sorts of thoughts and moods. . . . It's magnificent!"[99]

Overcome with Fears and Foreboding

Over the next several months they visited Rome while Scott did revisions on *The Great Gatsby.* Much of the winter Zelda was sick—first with colitis and then with ovarian problems. They were both drinking heavily and arguing bitterly.

When they left Rome for Paris in April 1925, Scott was edgy. The novel was going to be published that same month, and he was frantic with worry. This was the novel in which he had invested so much time and effort—more than his other work. Not

The Fitzgeralds seem more somber in this photograph taken after Zelda's marital infidelities.

only was he anxious for it to be liked by the critics, he was also counting on it to make money.

As soon as the book was released, the news from Maxwell Perkins in New York was mixed, as Scott learned when he reached Paris. The early critical reviews seemed very favorable. However, based on early tabulations, Perkins predicted disappointing sales for *The Great Gatsby*.

Scott was discouraged about the sales. He had hoped that he would not have to rely on publishing a volume of short stories, as he had after his other novels. He had counted on this novel's success to confirm his reputation as a serious novelist.

However, the book's first printing made him only $6,261—and $6,000 of that had to be repaid to Scribner's, since he had borrowed an advance. He wrote again to Perkins, reluctantly informing him that he did have a book of stories that could be published that fall. He planned to begin another novel, he told Perkins, and if that couldn't support him without "more intervals of trash," he vowed that he would give up, move to Hollywood, and write screenplays for movies. The financial insecurity, he complained, was killing him.

Meeting Hemingway

Though Scott was despondent about his bad luck with his latest novel, he was enthusiastic about seeking out another young American writer who was living in Paris, Ernest Hemingway. Back in October 1924, Edmund Wilson had read several of Hemingway's stories and poems and thought they were excellent. He told Scott to look Hemingway up whenever he got to Paris.

The two men shared a mutual respect. Hemingway was highly impressed with *The Great Gatsby*, calling it "an absolutely first-rate book." Scott was impressed with Hemingway, too—and quickly decided to help him get signed with Scribner's. "This is to tell you," Scott wrote to Maxwell Perkins, "about a young man named Ernest Hemingway, who lives in Paris, (an American). . . and has a brilliant future. . . . I'd look him up right away. He's the real thing." [100]

Scott's admiration was as much for the kind of man Hemingway was as for his writing talent, however. Since Scott was a teen, he had idolized war heroes and athletes, and Hemingway was both. "Six inches taller and forty pounds heavier than Fitzgerald, Hemingway was a literary version of the bloodied and bandaged football heroes Scott had worshiped in college," writes one biographer. "Hemingway had the masculine strength, capacity for drink, athletic prowess and experience in battle that Fitzgerald sadly lacked and desperately desired." [101]

Though friends, the two men were often critical of each other. Scott thought Hemingway tended to brag, especially about his experiences in the war. And Hemingway scorned Fitzgerald because he could not hold his liquor. He also was very suspicious of Zelda, who he thought was crazy, and he told Scott so.

Hemingway also believed that Zelda was jealous of her husband's talent and was sabotaging his writing by fostering his drinking. He told Scott years later how foolish he was to have married Zelda. "Of all people on earth you need discipline in your work," Hemingway said, "and instead you marry someone who is jealous of your work, wants to compete with you and ruins you." [102]

An Unsatisfactory Reaction

Fitzgerald heard from many of his friends after the publication of Tender Is the Night, *but Hemingway was not one of them. Puzzled and hurt, Fitzgerald wrote to his friend. The response he received, say some biographers, was fueled more by Hemingway's jealousy that occasionally surfaced than by any real literary criticism. The following is an excerpt from* Invented Lives: F. Scott and Zelda Fitzgerald *by James Mellow.*

"Fitzgerald had to wait for word from Hemingway; he did not hear from him during the serialization in *Scribner's Magazine.* Finally, on May 10, a month after the publication of *Tender is the Night,* Fitzgerald wrote, asking: 'Did you like the book? For God's sake, drop me a line and tell me one way or another. You can't hurt my feelings. I just want to get a few intelligent slants at it to get some of the reviewers' jargon out of my head.'

What he got from Hemingway was a long psychological critique of Fitzgerald's relation to his work, his professional attitudes, his personal involvement with the Murphys (to whom Fitzgerald had dedicated the book) . . . and of his marriage to Zelda. Hemingway began by saying he both liked *Tender is the Night* and didn't like it. He admired the marvelous description of Sara and Gerald [Murphy] with which Fitzgerald had started out. 'Then,' he commented, 'you started fooling with them, making them come from things they didn't come from, changing them into other people and you can't do that, Scott. . . . Goddam it, you took liberties with people's pasts and futures that produced not people but damned marvellously faked case histories.' His blunt opinion was that Fitzgerald had cheated with the book and that it had been unnecessary. Fitzgerald was too caught up in the good opinions of people . . . and too caught up in his family problems. 'Forget your personal tragedy,' he advised. 'We are all bitched from the start. . . . But when you get the damned hurt use it—don't cheat with it. . . . I'd like to see you and talk about things with you sober. . . . You were so damned stinking in N.Y. we didn't get anywhere. You see . . . you're not a tragic character. Neither am I. All we are is writers and what we should do is write.'"

Interestingly, Zelda was as hostile toward Hemingway. She felt he was a phony and called him "a professional he-man" or "a pansy with hair on his chest." [103]

"1,000 Parties and No Work"

The Fitzgeralds did continue an active social life. In Paris, and later in Antibes, interesting personalities abounded—among them John Dos Passos, Archibald MacLeish, and James Thurber. In addition, there were Sara and Gerald Murphy, an American couple the Fitzgeralds had grown close to during their time abroad. There were so many invitations and so much revelry that, in his journal, Scott referred to this time as one of "1,000 parties and no work." [104]

Hemingway, although certainly a part of the social scene in Europe, made sure it did not affect the time he set aside for writing each day. He criticized his friend, who, although he claimed to be working on a new novel called *Tender Is the Night*, seemed to have put his creative energy on hold.

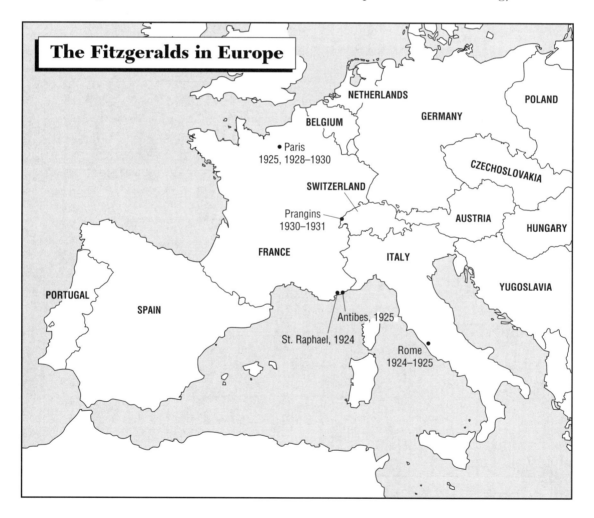

The Fitzgeralds in Europe

Ernest Hemingway (pictured) and F. Scott Fitzgerald became close friends while the two lived in Europe. Hemingway, however, criticized the younger writer for allowing his social excesses to interfere with his writing.

Parties seemed more interesting to Scott, but Hemingway felt as though Scott were wasting his talent and time. "I wonder," Hemingway chided Scott, "what your idea of heaven would be—A beautiful vacuum filled with wealthy monogamists all powerful and members of the best families all drinking themselves to death."[105]

Undeniably an Alcoholic

Scott's drinking was becoming more of a problem during this time, too. He was undeniably an alcoholic, which many of his friends were beginning to understand:

"Like many others who got the name of being drunkards," wrote one friend, "Scott simply couldn't drink. One cocktail and he was off. It seemed to affect him as much as five or six drinks affected Hemingway and myself. Immediately he was out of control and there was only one end . . . that he became thoroughly drunk, and like many Irishmen, when he became drunk he usually became very disagreeable and rude and quarrelsome, as if all his resentments were released at once."[106]

Hemingway was angry enough at Scott for the time he wasted drinking, but he became angrier still as his own life became

Advice to His Daughter

Although he was not physically or emotionally well enough to be very consistent in his relationship with Scottie when she was growing up, he tried to compensate somewhat by writing to her on a regular basis. In the following letter, sent in September 1938, Scott worries that as a Vassar student she will repeat some of the mistakes he had made at Princeton. The letter is included in F. Scott Fitzgerald: A Life in Letters, *edited by Matthew Bruccoli.*

"A chalk line is absolutely specified for you at present . . . beside the 'cleverness' which you are vaguely supposed to have 'inherited,' people will be quick to deck you out with my sins. If I hear of you taking a drink before you're twenty, I shall feel entitled to begin my last and greatest non-stop binge, and the world also will have an interest in the matter of your behavior. If you would like to be able to say, and would say on the slightest provocation: 'There she goes—just like her papa and mama.' Need I say that you can take this fact as a curse—or you can make of it a great advantage?

Remember that you're there for four years. It is a residential college and the butterfly will be resented. You should never boast to a soul that you're going to the Bachelors' Cotillion [a grand dance]. I can't tell you how important this is. For one hour of vainglory you will create a different attitude about yourself. Nothing as obnoxious as other people's luck. And while I'm on this: You will notice that there is a strongly organized left-wing movement there. I do not particularly want you to think about politics, but I do *not* want you to set yourself against this movement. I am known as a left-wing sympathizer, and would be proud if you were. In any case, I should feel outraged if you identified yourself with Nazism or Red-baiting in any form. Some of those radical girls may not look like much now but in your lifetime they are liable to be high in the councils of the nation."

affected. Scott would turn up at Hemingway's home in the evening after drinking or early in the morning after a night of partying. Years later, he would refuse to tell Scott his address, insisting instead that they meet in restaurants or cafes.

Scott was aware of his problem and would half-seriously greet strangers at parties by announcing that he was an alcoholic. In 1929 he confessed that drinking was becoming a way of life—and with it, a feeling of emptiness. "My latest tendency," he wrote, "is to collapse about 11:00 and, with the tears flowing from my eyes or the gin rising to their level and leaking over, tell interested friends or acquaintances that I haven't a friend in the world."[107]

Pranks and Worse

The drinking allowed his friends to glimpse a dark side to the glittery Jazz Age that Scott had once personified. The pranks he once pulled to amuse them had become immature, attention-getting devices that were increasingly hurtful and cruel.

For instance, once Scott and a few friends lured a hotel orchestra to his villa and locked them inside—forcing them to play a private concert. Another time, the same group captured a restaurant owner and several of the waiters and threatened to push them off a cliff.

More and more often he misbehaved at parties. When Gerald and Sara Murphy held a party in honor of Hemingway and his wife, Scott became jealous and surly. He threw ashtrays around the room, angering Gerald so much that he left his own party. Afterward Sara wrote to Scott, protesting his unfriendly attitude that ruined every party or gathering.

After another party at the Murphys' at which Scott punched Gerald, smashed Sara's prized glassware, and threw a fig at a visiting princess, he and Zelda were told they could not return to the Murphys' home for two weeks. Rather than express sorrow and embarrassment, however, Scott and Zelda stood outside the Murphys' villa the next time there was a party and threw armloads of garbage over the wall.

When the Fitzgeralds weren't causing a stir at a party, they were taking wild risks themselves. Their high-speed, alcohol-impaired car trips were perilous; on at least one occasion Scott turned off on a railroad trestle, parked, and went to sleep. If a farmer hadn't woken them early the next morning, they surely would have been killed.

Gerald Murphy later recalled that the Fitzgeralds seemed to be looking for something they couldn't find:

> I don't think it was parties that started Scott and Zelda on their adventures. . . . Their idea was that they never depended upon parties. I don't think they cared very much for parties, so called, and I don't think they stayed at them very long. They were all out, always searching for some kind of adventure *outside* of the party . . . it didn't . . . take a party to start them or anything of the kind. And they didn't stay around very much. They usually had their own funny little plans—they'd be with you for awhile and then they'd disappear and go on to some other place—and then you'd see them again somehow—they'd seek you out again.[108]

Changes in Zelda

The downward spiral of Scott's life was beginning to be mirrored in Zelda's, as well. Although she frequently joined him in his drunken escapades, she was not an alcoholic. She drank only to get a bit tipsy, and that enabled her to join in whatever "fun" was happening around her. The "fun," however, was becoming more unpredictable and self-destructive.

Several of the Fitzgeralds' friends sensed that Zelda was lonely and that she often felt left out. Scott's literary talent overshadowed her. Not since she left Montgomery to be married had she been the center of attention, and she missed that.

Her frustration—combined with Scott's drinking—often resulted in noisy quarrels, many times in front of friends. Zelda had a packed trunk ready just outside the door of their villa in case she decided to leave

Fitzgerald's alcoholism interfered with his writing and damaged his relationship with Zelda. As both continued to drink, their relationship became more self-destructive.

him. Sometimes she taunted him, accusing him of being cowardly, and dared him to perform dangerous tricks. On one occasion she challenged him to do a series of perilous high dives from a cliff into the sea; drunk, he accepted, as friends looked on in horror.

Zelda was also exhibiting suicidal tendencies. Once she lay down in front of their car and told Scott to run over her. (He would have, too, had friends not prevented him.) In another bizarre incident, Zelda threw herself down a flight of stone stairs after Scott had been paying attention to another woman at a cocktail party. Afterward, said friends, she wordlessly climbed back up and went to the washroom to clean off her skinned knees.

To Hollywood

The two and a half years in Europe seemed to go by quickly, although Scott had nothing to show for the time. He had not written his novel—in fact, he had not even written a short story. His health was poor (the constant smoking and drinking was having its effect), and his relationship with his wife was deteriorating. In December 1926 they sailed back to America, hoping to get their lives back on track, but it was not to be.

Scott was offered a job in Hollywood writing a script for a movie about college life. He would be paid $3,500, and if the script was accepted, he'd get another $12,000. The change of scene was intriguing for a very short while, but soon both he and Zelda tired of it.

Even though neither he nor Zelda was impressed by much in Hollywood, they still

Offered a job in Hollywood as a screenwriter, Fitzgerald failed to write a usable script but fell in love with eighteen-year-old starlet Lois Moran.

he and Zelda collected watches and other jewelry from the guests and boiled them in a pot of tomato soup. And at the home of legendary ladies' man, screenwriter John Monk Saunders, Zelda brandished a sharp pair of gardening shears and offered to castrate him, which she felt would greatly simplify his life. As always, many people were put off by these actions but were later forgiving because Scott could be so attractive when sober.

It was in Hollywood that Scott fell in love with an eighteen-year-old starlet named Lois Moran. Though it seems doubtful that they actually had an affair, Zelda was so bitter about her husband's flirtation that she started a fire in her hotel bathtub, burning all of her clothes. And when they left—United Artists declined Scott's script—they had another quarrel about Lois Moran, and Zelda threw the platinum and diamond watch she'd received from Scott years before out the train window.

Ellerslie—Another Failure

After the fiasco in Hollywood, Scott's publishers were becoming worried about the progress of his novel *Tender Is the Night*. As had been his habit for years, he'd been borrowing off future royalties for the book, but this novel seemed to be especially difficult for Scott to write.

In the spring of 1927 Maxwell Perkins suggested they find a quiet spot far from the parties in Great Neck and New York City. After a quick search, they found Ellerslie, a thirty-room mansion on the banks of the Delaware River, a few miles north of Wilmington. This, Scott decided, would be where he could complete his novel.

managed to find opportunities for parties and drinking. They also engaged in the same types of childish pranks they'd become notorious for elsewhere; at one party,

But the same temptations that followed them to Paris, to Great Neck, and elsewhere were there at Ellerslie. The fifteen large bedrooms and huge drawing rooms seemed to beg for occupants. The Fitzgeralds soon organized a series of riotous parties, with jazz bands brought in for entertainment.

Both Scott and Zelda wrote to everyone they knew, encouraging them to visit, and soon Ellerslie had acquired the dubious fame of drunken, well-attended, weekend chaos. At one party, several guests had an impromptu skeet-shooting competition using Zelda's best blue dishes, while others tried to play polo with croquet mallets on the backs of fat plow horses.

As the days drifted by in a haze of cigarette smoke and alcohol, work was forgotten; the novel lay, unfinished and jumbled, in a desk drawer.

Dancing Madness

It was during their time at Ellerslie that Zelda discovered her passion for ballet. Over the years she had always found something with which to busy herself—designing furniture for the house, making a dollhouse for Scottie, and even writing stories for women's magazines. (Such stories were

---

"Lamp in a Window"

Although Zelda's mental illness kept them from being together most of the time, Scott still considered Zelda the one true love of his life. In March 1935, he wrote a poem that was published by the New Yorker. *The poem, called "Lamp in a Window," is addressed to Zelda. It is included in Matthew Bruccoli's* Some Sort of Epic Grandeur: The Life of F. Scott Fitzgerald.

"Do you remember, before keys turned in locks
When life was a closeup, and not an occasional letter,
That I hated to swim naked from the rocks
While you liked absolutely nothing better?

Do you remember many hotel bureaus that had
Only three drawers? But the only bother
Was that each of us argued stubbornly, got mad
Trying to give the third one to the other.

East, west, the little car turned, often wrong
Up an erroneous Alp, an unmapped Savoy river,
We blamed each other, wild were our words and strong
And in an hour, laughed and called it liver.

And, though the end was desolate and unkind:
To turn the calendar at June and find December
On the next leaf; still stupid-got with grief, I find
These are the only quarrels that I can remember."

Zelda became obsessed with becoming a ballerina at the age of twenty-eight. She danced and practiced for hours with passionate intensity.

usually signed by Scott and published under his name, with Zelda's permission—she earned higher fees that way.)

However, at the age of twenty-eight, she became convinced that ballet dancing, which she had enjoyed as a child, was her true calling. With alarming single-mindedness, she chose a Russian teacher named Lubov Egorova and began her training. Zelda

worked at ballet with an intensity that one friend described as "like the dancing madness of the Middle Ages." [109]

She was a woman obsessed, convinced that she could achieve greatness if only she could practice a few more hours longer than the previous day, spend a little more time at the barre doing her exercises. When she wasn't at her class, she was practicing at home in front of the mirror, the gramophone scratching out music incessantly. She danced when she was alone, and she danced when the house was filled with guests. Nothing mattered more than her dancing.

Gerald and Sara Murphy, who had always been fiercely loyal to Zelda, were nervous that she was pushing both her mind and her body far beyond what they could bear. Looking back years later, the Murphys and others close to Zelda could see that her obsession with dancing was an early signal of her mental illness—the confusion and madness from which she would never recover. In 1928, however, it seemed just one more impulsive, crazy aspect of the Fitzgeralds' already chaotic lives.

8 Falling Apart

Zelda's first breakdown occurred in April 1930 when they were in Paris. They had been on the move during the past two years, back and forth between Ellerslie and Paris, the Riviera, and even a sightseeing trip to Algiers. Zelda was incoherent and exhausted, and she was hearing voices. Doctors diagnosed her as schizophrenic and explained that her collapse was inevitable. Scott placed her in a clinic in Switzerland, hoping doctors could cure her.

"I Left My Capacity for Hoping"

Zelda was well enough to leave the clinic and return to the United States in the fall of 1931, although she was certainly not the young woman she had been. She is almost unrecognizable in photographs taken after her release—her once-delicate features now seemed coarse and hard. "Her hair was roughly cut," writes one observer, "her clothes plain; and she now looked institutional rather than chic."[110]

It was less than four months before she had a second collapse. Zelda herself recognized that she was ill, and she was admitted to the Phipps Psychiatric Clinic in Baltimore. Her condition—often marked by both se-

vere depression and anxiety—did not improve much. Scott decided to rent a house, known as La Paix, nearby so that he and Scottie could see her occasionally. He spent his time trying to remain sober—without success—and finish his novel *Tender Is the Night*.

By that summer, Zelda appeared well enough to be able to spend time at the house with Scott and Scottie. However, it was soon clear that she was not recovering. At La Paix, Zelda inexplicably tried to burn some clothes in an unused fireplace on the second floor and set the house on fire.

When she had her third breakdown early in 1934, optimism for an eventual recovery had disappeared. Doctors knew that each breakdown in a schizophrenic made a happy ending less likely. Fitzgerald wrote later, "I left my capacity for hoping on the little roads that led to Zelda's sanitarium."[111]

Tender Is the Night

While Zelda was in and out of hospitals and clinics, Scott was fighting his own demons. He was frustrated at his inability to make progress on his novel at a time when he needed money the most, for Zelda's treatment was extremely expensive. In addition,

Zelda's Last Days

Zelda Fitzgerald out-lived her husband by a little more than seven years. Although usually confined to the sanitarium, she occasionally was allowed short visits to see Scottie or to visit her mother in Mont-gomery. In the follow-ing excerpt from F. Scott Fitzgerald: A Biography, *Andre Le Vot discusses the tragic circumstances of her death.*

"Zelda seemed not to have been as shattered by her husband's death as might have been feared. In fact, as had happened when her father died, it was months before she felt the blow. Then she had to return to Highland for awhile. She continued to write and paint, was subject to spells of mysticism, lived apart from the world. . . . Zelda did not attend Scottie's marriage in February 1943 to Lieutenant Samuel J. Lanahan in New York, but she was uprooted by the birth of her first grandchild three years later. . . .

In November 1947, shortly before her second grandchild was born, she had to return to the hospi-tal. Six months later, on the night of March 10–11, the hospital's main building, in which she and thirty other patients were housed, caught fire. . . . Locked in her room on the top floor, she and nine other women died in the flames. Her body was identified through a dental examination."

his production of short stories, on which he'd always relied for quick cash, was de-creasing. Those stories he did complete were often poorly written—more like rough drafts than finished works—and his agent was unable to sell them to the magazines that had formerly sought his work.

The cause—as well as the result—of most of these frustrations was alcohol. He drank when he couldn't write, he drank when he couldn't concentrate, and he drank when he was angry. As a result, the quality of his work suffered, which made him more de-spondent, and the drinking would increase.

When he finally did finish *Tender Is the Night,* the results were disappointing. He had hoped the book would make him money, but its sales didn't even cover the advances he had been paid by Scribner's. Although many critics liked the book, it was not the type of story people wanted to hear. The novel, as always autobiog-raphical, drew heavily on the painful episodes of his recent life—Zelda's break-down, his drinking, and the lifestyle of the idle rich living on the Riviera. But because Americans were mired in the Depression, such a story seemed outdated and crass. Reviewers criticized the book as "a rather irritating type of chic," with a "clever and brilliant surface but . . . not wise and ma-ture."[112]

"Even If There Isn't Any Me"

Scott was depressed about the cool reception of his novel in 1934; he also was more and more worried about Zelda. Throughout her years of hospitalization, she had always had times when her mind seemed to clear. Sometimes during these episodes, Scott would take her on a short trip or for

Zelda and Scott Fitzgerald attend the Baltimore opening of Dinner at Eight *in 1932. From 1930 on, Zelda would be in and out of mental hospitals.*

a visit with old friends. However, such episodes were increasingly rare now. She hallucinated and was furious when others couldn't hear the voices that she heard. She attempted suicide several times—once by dashing in front of a train when she was out walking with Scott. His quick action prevented a horrible death.

They saw each other less and less, but they continued to write letters. In one, Zelda apologized for her illness, which she admits ruined their lives:

> Now that there isn't any more happiness and home is gone and there isn't even any past and no emotions but those that were yours where there could be my comfort—it is a shame that we should have met in harshness and coldness where there was once so much tenderness and so many dreams. . . . I love you anyway—even if there isn't any me or any love or even any life.[113]

Even so, he continued to visit her whenever her doctors allowed. He still considered her the most important woman he'd ever known. After visiting her one afternoon, Scott wrote that they still had a powerful bond that could never be broken: "It was wonderful to sit with her head on my shoulder for hours and feel as I always have even now, closer to her than to any other human being."[114]

Hitting Bottom

As Zelda's mental health deteriorated, Scott's physical health was failing. He had been diagnosed years before with a mild form of tuberculosis; in May 1935 doctors told him that his lungs were worse. He needed care and was sent to Asheville, North Carolina, to a center for pulmonary disease.

Those who saw Scott then noted that he was visibly ill. He smoked and drank constantly, was dependent on pills to sleep, and could not write even a line.

Doctors advised him to give up his drinking, but the best he could do was switch from gin to beer. To get the same amount of alcohol as he had gotten from gin, he had to drink huge amounts of beer—between thirty-five and thirty-eight bottles each day. His room was a mass of beer bottles. There were cases jammed under the beds and stacked in the bathtub. The cases served as tables for his paper, manuscripts, and cigarettes.

After a while the beer was too much trouble, so he went back to gin, and the heavy drinking took its toll on his already wasted frame. He looked more like a man of seventy than of forty. His skin was raw and waxy; he could not hold down solid food because of the damage to his liver. Even walking was a problem—he was forced to hold on to the furniture when he crossed the room. He suffered from hallucinations caused by heavy drinking, too. He once told a good friend—"in full skin-crawling detail—how in 1935 he saw beetles and pink mice scurrying all over him and elephants dancing on the ceiling."[115]

"The Crack-Up"

Scott had hit rock bottom, and he knew it. He was sick, chemically dependent, and broke. By his own calculations, he owed more than $40,000—either to kindhearted friends or to Maxwell Perkins for advances on his books.

Because of his drinking, the quality of his writing had slipped even further, and Scribner's now refused to advance him any money, realizing it was unlikely they'd ever get it back. Scott was staying in a dollar-a-night hotel, spending almost nothing on food. It was a far cry, he noted, from the style to which he and Zelda had grown accustomed. "I am living very cheaply," he wrote in his journal. "Today I am in comparative affluence, but Monday and Tuesday I had two tins of potted meat, three oranges, and a box of Uneedas [crackers] and two cans of beer. The food totaled 18 cents a day—and I think of the thousand meals I've sent back untasted in the last two years."[116]

He waited for some inspiration—an idea for a novel, a short story—but nothing came. He wrote nonfiction—the first he'd ever done, although most of his writing was based on his own experiences. He sold *Esquire* magazine a three-part series about his hitting bottom—his drinking, his illness, and even his frantic hope that an idea would come to him in the middle of the night.

The essays were well written and were praised by critics for their honesty. But the reaction of his friends—particularly other writers—was largely negative. Maxwell Perkins thought the articles were embarrassing and wished that Scott had not written them, while Hemingway thought the highly personal admissions of failure were shameful.

Hollywood, One More Time

In July 1937, Metro-Goldwyn-Mayer (MGM) in Hollywood offered Scott a contract to write screenplays. He was elated; MGM

A Portrait of an Author

In Jeffrey Meyers's book Scott Fitzgerald: A Biography, *he gives a description of Fitzgerald at the age of forty— aged and weary with the effects of disease and alcoholism.*

"Sheila [Graham] described the handsome but rather sad and weary Fitzgerald, who was forty when they met, as having 'hair pale blond, a wide attractive forehead, grey-blue eyes set far apart, set beautifully in his head, a straight, sharply chiseled nose and an expressive mouth that seemed to sag a little at the corners, giving the face a gently melancholy expression.' His hair was thinning on top and he carefully combed it over his bald patch. Aware that tuberculosis (which had killed [Sheila's] father) was infectious, he warned her not to use the same cutlery and dishes as he did. . . . His craving for sweets, when he gave up alcohol, was insatiable; he drank endless Coca-Colas and gorged himself on fudge. He also went in for exotic dishes like turtle soup and chocolate *souffle*. Insomniac and addicted to barbiturates, he took a heavy dose of chloral and two or more Nembutals to put himself to sleep, and needed several benzedrine pills to wake up."

As Zelda's mental health deteriorated, Scott's physical health began to worsen from years of alcoholism.

Fitzgerald was offered a screenwriting job for MGM in 1937. Although Fitzgerald desperately needed the money the job paid, he was unable to write a successful script.

would pay him the exorbitant amount of $1,000 a week, and he desperately needed the money. Scottie was in private school, and because he refused to put Zelda in a public insane asylum, her care was extremely expensive, too.

Six months before he had been totally demoralized, but he went to Hollywood eager and hopeful. Even so, friends who saw Scott there noticed what a change had come over him. He seemed shy, insecure, and completely without confidence. Scott recognized these traits in himself, too. In a letter to Maxwell Perkins, he knew that he seemed to be merely going through the motions. "Five years have rolled away from me," Scott wrote, "and I can't decide exactly who I am, if anyone."[117]

A Different Measure of Success

As things turned out, Scott had no more success at MGM than he had had at United Artists. He was assigned to write a script for a movie called *Three Comrades,* starring Robert Taylor and Margaret Sullivan. He prepared conscientiously for the assignment, viewing dozens of old movies to understand the plot and format. He bought books on the craft of screenwriting, poring over them into the late hours of the night.

But again, he failed. He was, remembered director Billy Wilder, like "a great sculptor who is hired to do a plumbing job. He did not know how to connect the pipes so the water would flow." [118] Though no one could dispute his abilities as a novelist, his talents did not carry over to screenwriting. He especially had trouble with dialogue; although he could write dialogue that read well on the printed page, it didn't sound realistic when spoken. As a result, most of his work had to be rewritten—a fact that infuriated him.

He helped on other movies, but he was no more successful with any of them than he had been with *Three Comrades.* In December 1938 he was fired by MGM. Although he was angry and hurt, he had to admit that he had achieved some measure of success in his work—he had made a great deal of money in a year and a half and was able to pay off all of his debts.

The End of Things

After leaving MGM he began writing, once again, for himself. He was working on a novel called *The Last Tycoon,* based on the movie producer Irving Thalberg. His health was poor, however, and writing was more of a struggle than it ever had been before. Sheila Graham, a Hollywood newspaper columnist with whom he had a close relationship, was helping him remain sober.

"I can't exercise even a little any more," he wrote to Scottie, now in college. "I'm best off in my room." [119] He also continued writing to Zelda, assuring her that it felt good to be writing again.

In November 1940 he was in a nearby drugstore buying a pack of cigarettes when he suffered a mild heart attack. His doctor

Hollywood columnist Sheila Graham developed a close relationship with Fitzgerald. She was with him on the day of his death in 1940.

advised bed rest, and though Scott complied, he continued to write. He felt confident about his novel; although his health dictated a much slower writing schedule, he assured Maxwell Perkins that *The Last Tycoon* would be finished in January.

He never finished the book. On December 21, while reading the *Princeton Alumni Weekly* and eating a Hershey bar, he suddenly stood up and clutched the mantlepiece. He fell to the floor, breathing heavily. Sheila, who was in the room at the time,

---

"He Was Terribly Nervous"

Late in 1939 an ill, exhausted Fitzgerald had a visit from his friend, writer John O'Hara, and he allowed O'Hara a first look at his novel-in-progress, The Last Tycoon. *O'Hara's memories of that afternoon are recorded by Matthew Bruccoli in* Some Sort of Epic Grandeur: The Life of F. Scott Fitzgerald.

"He was terribly nervous, disappearing for five and ten minutes at a time, once to get a plaid tie to give my wife because she was wearing a Glen plaid suit. Once to get a volume of Thackeray because I'd never read Thackeray, another time to get some tome about Julius Caesar which he assured me was scholarly yet readable—but which he knew I would never read.

Then we went out and took some pictures, and when we finished that he suddenly said, 'Would you like to read what I've written, but first promise you won't tell anyone about it. Don't tell them anything. Don't tell them what it's about, or anything about the people. I'd like it better if you didn't even tell anyone I'm writing another novel.'

So we went back to the house and I read what he had written. He saw that I was comfortable, with pillows, cigarettes, ashtrays, a coke. And sat there tortured, trying to be casual, but unhappy because he did not know that my deadpan was partly due to my being an extremely slow reader of good writing, and partly because this *was* such good writing that I was reading. When I had read it I said, 'Scott, don't take any more movie jobs until you've finished this. You work so slowly and this is so good, you've got to finish it. It's real Fitzgerald.'

Then, of course, he became blasphemous and abusive, and asked me if I wanted to fight. I saw him a few times after that day, and once when I asked him how the book was coming, he only said, 'You've kept your promise? You haven't spoken to anyone about it?'"

frantically called the police and the fire department. By the time they arrived, however, Fitzgerald was dead.

"You Can Take Off Your Hats Now, Gentlemen"

Edmund Wilson edited the unfinished manuscript of *The Last Tycoon* after his friend's death, convinced that it was Scott's "most mature piece of work" even in its incomplete state. Many agreed with his assessment when the book was released in October 1941. James Thurber wrote, "Fitzgerald's perfection of style and form . . . has a way of making something that lies between your stomach and your heart quiver a little." [120]

But Fitzgerald's skill as an author had been marred by his lifestyle. For many people it was difficult to separate the man—with his often boorish, drunken behavior—from his writing. Even before the time of his death he had become the symbol of an almost embarrassing time in American history—a time of excess and glitter without substance. Those excesses were obvious in the way he and Zelda had lived their lives, and when the frantic energy for which they were famous finally ran out, Scott's talent was largely forgotten.

However, time has been good to F. Scott Fitzgerald. His works are read far more now than they were during his lifetime. He is not only the spokesman for his generation—as he was in the 1920s—but an example of one whose life was entangled with his writing. Some critics noted that Fitzgerald had lived the life he wrote about so intensely that he was broken by it.

Fitzgerald continues to be considered one of America's greatest writers for his depiction of the Jazz Age of the 1920s.

Yet however tragic a figure he was, there is a great achievement in his writing, as Stephen Vincent Benet proclaimed in his review of *The Last Tycoon*. "You can take off your hats now, gentlemen, and I think perhaps you had better. This is not a legend, this is a reputation—and seen in perspective, it may well be one of the most secure reputations of our time." [121]

Notes

Introduction: Praise, Scorn, and Pity

1. Quoted in Matthew Bruccoli and Jackson Bryer, eds., *F. Scott Fitzgerald in His Own Time: A Miscellany.* Kent, OH: Kent State University Press, 1971, pp. 310–11.

2. Garrison Keillor, "Greeting," in *Fitzgerald: A Commemorative Publication.* St. Paul, MN: Primarius Limited, September 1996, p. 4.

3. Quoted in Matthew J. Bruccoli, *Some Sort of Epic Grandeur: The Life of F. Scott Fitzgerald.* New York: Harcourt Brace Jovanovich, 1981, p. 6.

4. Quoted in Jeffrey Meyers, *Scott Fitzgerald: A Biography.* New York: HarperCollins, 1994, p. 334.

5. Quoted in Meyers, *Scott Fitzgerald,* p. 334.

6. Quoted in Bruccoli and Bryer, *In His Own Time,* p. 470.

7. Quoted in James R. Mellow, *Invented Lives: F. Scott and Zelda Fitzgerald.* Boston: Houghton Mifflin, 1984, p. 489.

8. Quoted in Bruccoli and Bryer, *In His Own Time,* p. 472.

9. Terese Zech, interview with Gail B. Stewart, St. Paul, MN, September 3, 1998.

Chapter 1: Minnesota Roots

10. Quoted in Meyers, *Scott Fitzgerald,* p. 5.

11. Arthur Mizener, *Scott Fitzgerald.* New York: G. P. Putnam's Sons, 1972, p. 5.

12. Quoted in Dave Page and John Koblas, *F. Scott Fitzgerald in Minnesota: Toward the Summit.* St. Cloud, MN: North Star Press of St. Cloud, 1996, p. 20.

13. Quoted in Page and Koblas, *F. Scott Fitzgerald in Minnesota,* p. 20.

14. Quoted in Meyers, *Scott Fitzgerald,* p. 6.

15. Quoted in Scott Donaldson, *Fool for Love: F. Scott Fitzgerald.* New York: Congdon and Weed, 1983, pp. 9, 16.

16. Quoted in Mellow, *Invented Lives,* p. 13.

17. Quoted in Meyers, *Scott Fitzgerald,* p. 7.

18. Quoted in Meyers, *Scott Fitzgerald,* p. 9.

19. Quoted in Meyers, *Scott Fitzgerald,* p. 9.

Chapter 2: The Seeds of a Writing Life

20. Quoted in Bruccoli, *Some Sort of Epic Grandeur,* p. 23.

21. Quoted in Bruccoli, *Some Sort of Epic Grandeur,* p. 25.

22. Quoted in Katie de Koster, ed., *Readings on F. Scott Fitzgerald.* San Diego: Greenhaven Press, 1998, p. 14.

23. Quoted in Bruccoli, *Some Sort of Epic Grandeur,* p. 26.

24. Quoted in Bruccoli, *Some Sort of Epic Grandeur,* p. 28.

25. Quoted in Page and Koblas, *F. Scott Fitzgerald in Minnesota,* p. 29.

26. Quoted in Bruccoli, *Some Sort of Epic Grandeur,* p. 27.

27. Quoted in Meyers, *Scott Fitzgerald,* pp. 11–12.

28. Quoted in Page and Koblas, *F. Scott Fitzgerald in Minnesota,* p. 52.

29. Quoted in Page and Koblas, *F. Scott Fitzgerald in Minnesota,* p. 52.

30. Quoted in Andre Le Vot, *F. Scott Fitzgerald: A Biography.* Garden City, NY: Doubleday, 1983, pp. 18–19.

31. Quoted in Bruccoli, *Some Sort of Epic Grandeur,* p. 29.

32. Quoted in Meyers, *Scott Fitzgerald,* p. 14.

33. Quoted in Meyers, *Scott Fitzgerald,* p. 15.

34. Quoted in Le Vot, *F. Scott Fitzgerald,* p. 22.

35. Quoted in Meyers, *Scott Fitzgerald,* p. 33.

36. Quoted in Bruccoli and Bryer, *In His Own Time,* p. 3.

37. Quoted in Le Vot, *F. Scott Fitzgerald,* p. 23.

38. Quoted in Meyers, *Scott Fitzgerald,* p. 17.

Chapter 3: Away to Princeton

39. Quoted in Bruccoli, *Some Sort of Epic Grandeur,* p. 33.

40. Quoted in Bruccoli, *Some Sort of Epic Grandeur,* pp. 39–40.

41. Le Vot, *F. Scott Fitzgerald,* p. 46.

42. Quoted in Le Vot, *F. Scott Fitzgerald,* pp. 32–33.

43. Quoted in Meyers, *Scott Fitzgerald,* p. 22.

44. Quoted in Mizener, *Scott Fitzgerald,* p. 23.

45. Quoted in Bruccoli, *Some Sort of Epic Grandeur,* p. 68.

46. Quoted in Meyers, *Scott Fitzgerald,* p. 23.

47. Quoted in Bruccoli, *Some Sort of Epic Grandeur,* p. 46.

48. Quoted in Le Vot, *F. Scott Fitzgerald,* p. 39.

49. Quoted in Bruccoli, *Some Sort of Epic Grandeur,* p. 49.

50. Quoted in Le Vot, *F. Scott Fitzgerald,* p. 40.

51. Quoted in Bruccoli and Bryer, *In His Own Time,* pp. 7–8.

52. Quoted in Le Vot, *F. Scott Fitzgerald,* p. 52.

53. Quoted in Bruccoli, *Some Sort of Epic Grandeur,* p. 55.

54. Quoted in Meyers, *Scott Fitzgerald,* p. 30.

55. Quoted in Meyers, *Scott Fitzgerald,* p. 29.

56. Quoted in Mizener, *Scott Fitzgerald,* pp. 30–31.

57. Quoted in Page and Koblas, *F. Scott Fitzgerald in Minnesota,* p. 85.

Chapter 4: War and Zelda

58. Quoted in Meyers, *Scott Fitzgerald,* p. 34.

59. Quoted in Meyers, *Scott Fitzgerald,* p. 35.

60. Quoted in Meyers, *Scott Fitzgerald,* p. 36.

61. Quoted in Mellow, *Invented Lives,* p. 48.

62. Quoted in Mellow, *Invented Lives,* p. 56.

63. Quoted in Donaldson, *Fool for Love,* p. 61.

64. Quoted in Meyers, *Scott Fitzgerald,* p. 44.

65. Quoted in Bruccoli, *Some Sort of Epic Grandeur,* p. 90.

66. Quoted in Le Vot, *F. Scott Fitzgerald,* p. 64.

67. Quoted in Meyers, *Scott Fitzgerald,* p. 46.

68. Quoted in Le Vot, *F. Scott Fitzgerald,* p. 66.

69. Quoted in Meyers, *Scott Fitzgerald,* p. 48.

70. Quoted in Mizener, *Scott Fitzgerald,* p. 38.

71. Quoted in Le Vot, *F. Scott Fitzgerald,* p. 67.

72. Quoted in Mellow, *Invented Lives,* p. 61.

73. Quoted in Bruccoli, *Some Sort of Epic Grandeur,* p. 96.

74. Quoted in Donaldson, *Fool for Love,* p. 67.

75. Quoted in Le Vot, *F. Scott Fitzgerald,* p. 68.

76. Quoted in Le Vot, *F. Scott Fitzgerald,* p. 69.

77. Quoted in Mellow, *Invented Lives,* pp. 69, 70–71.

Chapter 5: Early Success

78. Quoted in Kate Moos, "1919: St. Paul, Minnesota," in *Fitzgerald: A Commemorative Publication,* p. 18.

79. Quoted in Mellow, *Invented Lives,* p. 72.

80. Quoted in Bruccoli, *Some Sort of Epic Grandeur,* p. 103.

81. Quoted in Bruccoli, *Some Sort of Epic Grandeur,* p. 103.

82. Quoted in Bruccoli, *Some Sort of Epic Grandeur,* p. 105.

83. Quoted in Mizener, *Scott Fitzgerald,* p. 46.

84. Quoted in Le Vot, *F. Scott Fitzgerald,* p. 73.

85. Quoted in Mellow, *Invented Lives,* p. 85.

86. Quoted in Mellow, *Invented Lives,* p. 86.

87. Quoted in Joan M. Allen, *Candles and Carnival Lights: The Catholic Sensibility of F. Scott Fitzgerald.* New York: New York University Press, 1978, pp. 61–62.

88. Quoted in Le Vot, *F. Scott Fitzgerald,* p. 76.

89. Quoted in de Koster, *Readings on F. Scott Fitzgerald,* p. 25.

Chapter 6: Fame and Fortune

90. Mizener, *Scott Fitzgerald,* pp. 53–54.

91. Le Vot, *F. Scott Fitzgerald*, p. 73.

92. Quoted in Bruccoli, *Some Sort of Epic Grandeur*, p. 151.

93. Quoted in Bruccoli, *Some Sort of Epic Grandeur*, p. 151.

94. Quoted in Bruccoli, *Some Sort of Epic Grandeur*, p. 150.

95. Quoted in Le Vot, *F. Scott Fitzgerald*, p. 90.

96. Quoted in Mizener, *Scott Fitzgerald*, p. 66.

97. Le Vot, *F. Scott Fitzgerald*, p. 174.

98. Quoted in Bruccoli, *Some Sort of Epic Grandeur*, p. 199.

Chapter 7: The Unraveling

99. Quoted in Bruccoli, *Some Sort of Epic Grandeur*, p. 213.

100. Quoted in Meyers, *Scott Fitzgerald*, pp. 130, 139.

101. Meyers, *Scott Fitzgerald*, p. 134.

102. Quoted in Meyers, *Scott Fitzgerald*, p. 148.

103. Quoted in Bruccoli, *Some Sort of Epic Grandeur*, p. 229.

104. Quoted in Mizener, *Scott Fitzgerald*, p. 72.

105. Quoted in Bruccoli, *Some Sort of Epic Grandeur*, p. 229.

106. Quoted in Meyers, *Scott Fitzgerald*, p. 147.

107. Quoted in Meyers, *Scott Fitzgerald*, p. 144.

108. Quoted in Bruccoli, *Some Sort of Epic Grandeur*, pp. 254–55.

109. Quoted in Mizener, *Scott Fitzgerald*, p. 81.

Chapter 8: Falling Apart

110. Meyers, *Scott Fitzgerald*, p. 213.

111. Quoted in Mizener, *Scott Fitzgerald*, p. 90.

112. Quoted in Mizener, *Scott Fitzgerald*, p. 92.

113. Quoted in Meyers, *Scott Fitzgerald*, p. 250.

114. Quoted in Meyers, *Scott Fitzgerald*, p. 250.

115. Quoted in Meyers, *Scott Fitzgerald*, p. 261.

116. Quoted in Meyers, *Scott Fitzgerald*, p. 259.

117. Quoted in Mizener, *Scott Fitzgerald*, p. 101.

118. Quoted in Meyers, *Scott Fitzgerald*, p. 291.

119. Quoted in Mizener, *Scott Fitzgerald*, p. 105.

120. Quoted in Bruccoli, *Some Sort of Epic Grandeur*, p. 492.

121. Quoted in Bruccoli, *Some Sort of Epic Grandeur*, p. 494.

For Further Reading

Nelson Manfred Blake, *Novelists' America: Fiction as History, 1910–1940*. Syracuse, NY: Syracuse University Press, 1969. Good chapter on life in the Jazz Age.

Tony Buttitta, *After the Gay Good Times: Asheville—Summer of '35: A Season with F. Scott Fitzgerald*. New York: Viking Press, 1974. Interesting material on Fitzgerald's battles with alcoholism.

William F. Fahey, *F. Scott Fitzgerald and the American Dream*. New York: Thomas Y. Crowell, 1973. Good index; helpful information on Fitzgerald's place among authors of his day.

F. Scott Fitzgerald, *Afternoon of an Author*. New York: Charles Scribner's Sons, 1957. Includes essays by the author—a glimpse into his day-to-day life.

Lloyd Hackl, *F. Scott Fitzgerald and St. Paul: "Still Home to Me."* Cambridge, MN: Adventure Publications, 1996. Superb collection of photographs of his childhood neighborhood and friends.

Nancy Milford, *Zelda Fitzgerald: A Biography*. New York: Harper and Row, 1970. Fascinating information on Zelda's family background.

Francis Kroll Ring, *Against the Current: As I Remember F. Scott Fitzgerald*. Berkeley, CA: Creative Arts, 1985. Interesting perspective of Fitzgerald; easy reading.

Works Consulted

Joan M. Allen, *Candles and Carnival Lights: The Catholic Sensibility of F. Scott Fitzgerald.* New York: New York University Press, 1978. Interesting information on Fitzgerald's changing attitudes on religion; good introduction.

Matthew J. Bruccoli, *Some Sort of Epic Grandeur: The Life of F. Scott Fitzgerald.* New York: Harcourt Brace Jovanovich, 1981. Excellent notes; helpful bibliography.

Matthew Bruccoli, ed., *F. Scott Fitzgerald: A Life in Letters.* New York: Charles Scribner's Sons, 1994. Invaluable index.

Matthew Bruccoli and Jackson Bryer, eds., *F. Scott Fitzgerald in His Own Time: A Miscellany.* Kent, OH: Kent State University Press, 1971. Helpful collection, especially of Fitzgerald's earliest work.

Matthew Bruccoli and Margaret Duggan, eds., *The Correspondence of F. Scott Fitzgerald.* New York: Random House, 1980. Extremely helpful in understanding his relationships with his wife and daughter.

Katie de Koster, ed., *Readings on F. Scott Fitzgerald.* San Diego: Greenhaven Press, 1998. Helpful literary criticism of his novels; good bibliography.

Scott Donaldson, *Fool for Love: F. Scott Fitzgerald.* New York: Congdon and Weed, 1983. Excellent section on Mollie Fitzgerald's relationship with her son.

Fitzgerald: A Commemorative Publication. St. Paul, MN: Primarius Limited, September 1996. Helpful for getting a modern appraisal of Fitzgerald in his hometown.

Sheila Graham, *The Real F. Scott Fitzgerald: Thirty-Five Years Later.* New York: Grosset and Dunlap, 1976. Includes fascinating information on Fitzgerald's relationship with his daughter, Scottie.

Andre Le Vot, *F. Scott Fitzgerald: A Biography.* Garden City, NY: Doubleday, 1983. Good background material on Princeton.

James R. Mellow, *Invented Lives: F. Scott and Zelda Fitzgerald.* Boston: Houghton Mifflin, 1984. Helpful footnotes and index.

Jeffrey Meyers, *Scott Fitzgerald: A Biography.* New York: HarperCollins, 1994. Readable source, excellent section on his courtship of Zelda.

Arthur Mizener, *The Far Side of Paradise: A Biography of F. Scott Fitzgerald.* Boston: Houghton Mifflin, 1965. Excellent index and source list.

Arthur Mizener, *Scott Fitzgerald.* New York: G. P. Putnam's Sons, 1972. Excellent photographs; very readable account of his life.

Dave Page and John Koblas, *F. Scott Fitzgerald in Minnesota: Toward the Summit.* St. Cloud, MN: North Star Press of St. Cloud, 1996. Excellent quotes and detail, especially about his early years in St. Paul.

Index

Picture Credits

About the Author

Gail B. Stewart received her undergraduate degree from Gustavus Adolphus College in St. Peter, Minnesota. She did her graduate work in English, linguistics, and curriculum study at the College of St. Thomas and the University of Minnesota. She taught English and reading for more than ten years.

She has written over ninety books for young people, including a series for Lucent Books called The Other America. She has written many books on historical topics such as World War I and the Warsaw Ghetto.

Stewart and her husband live in Minneapolis with their three sons, Ted, Elliot, and Flynn, two dogs, and a cat. When she is not writing she enjoys reading, walking, and watching her sons play soccer.